POLITICAL DEVELOPMENT IN NEPAL

Political Development in Nepal

Edited by

B. R. BAJRACHARYA
S. R. SHARMA
S. R. BAKHSI

ANMOL PUBLICATIONS PVT LTD
New Delhi—110 002

ANMOL PUBLICATIONS PVT LTD
4374/4B, Ansari Road
Darya Ganj, New Delhi-110 002

First Edition, 1993

ISBN 81-7041-844-5

Printed in India

Published by J. L. Kumar for Anmol Publications Pvt. Ltd., New Delhi and Printed at Amit Enterprises, 518/14, Anup Market, Maujpur, Delhi.

Preface

Nepal was formed with the amalgamation of many tiny Himalayan states by Prithvinarayan Shah, who proclaimed himself as a king after conquering these states. A period soon started, when the Rana family acquired real political power as Prime Minister, which became a hereditary power.

With the help of the Indian Prime Minister Jawahar Lal Nehru, the captive king Tribhuvan, became free in 1951 when he acquired power from the Prime Minister after fleeing to India as a fugitive. Latu King Mahendra became more autocratic and tried to distance himself from India and went closer to China, at that time an adversary of India.

The democratic forces were crushed and parliament dissolved and the leaders of Nepali Congress were arrested. After his death the present king Birendra has shown wisdom and moderation and has transferred powers to the people's representatives. A parliamentary form of Government headed by G. P. Koirala has been established which is friendly to India.

All these developments have been discussed in this book.

The editors feel grateful to the staff of the Library of Indian Council of World Affairs at Sapru House and the staff of the Nehru Memorial Museum Library, Teen Murthi House for their kind assistance in the preparation of this book.

EDITORS

Contents

Contents

1

Introduction

The Panchayat Polity in Nepal

Before the 1962 Constitution became effective, three independent but interrelated tiers of institutions had been created—first, a Panchayat framework consisting of the Town or the Village, the District and the Zonal Panchayats; second, the class organization structure, including the Women's Organization, Peasants' Organization, Labour Organization, Youth Organization, and Ex-Servicemen's Organization; and third, the Ministry of National Guidance to supervise the working and affairs of the Panchayats and the class organizations. Many sections of the 1962 Constitution suffered from a lack of detail, because the important institutions it provided for had already been set up by legislation and had been in existence for some time before the Constitution itself came into force. The Constitution sought to weld the already existing institutions and procedures into a coherent and integrated mechanism. However, the 1962 Constitution cannot be properly analysed and understood except in the light of the relevant supplementary legislation and the manner in which it has been implemented.

The four-tier Panchayat framework consisted of the Village Panchayat, the District Panchayat, the Zonal Panchayat (which was subsequently replaced by the Zonal Committee of the King's nominees), together with their respective Assemblies or Sabhas, and the Rastriya Panchayat (National Legislature) at the highest level. The Rastriya Panchayat resembles an assembly in functions and character rather than the Panchayats at the lower level, which are essentially executive committees or councils. With the exception of the Village (Gaun) or the Town (Nagar) Panchayat which is directly elected by a Village Assembly (Gaun Sabha) compounded of the adult population in the village, all other panchayats or Assemblies in the Panchayat hierarchy were indirectly elected. District Assemblies (Zilla Sabhas) were made up of representatives from the Village Panchayats, one from each village in the district. This Assembly elected from among its members an 11-member District Panchayat. All the members of all the District Panchayats in a particular zone constituted the Zonal Assembly (Anchal Sabha) whose members, together with the Chairman and Vice-Chairman, formed the electoral colleges to elect members from various districts of the zone to the Rastriya Panchayat.

Although the Panchayat system, at least in theory, provided a structure on a popular base, it had an extremely limited range of political participation. The total membership of Nepal's national legislature, the Rastriya Panchayat, was one hundred and twenty-five. It included 16 nominees of the King. Of the 109 elected members, 90 were elected by the 14 Zonal Assemblies as described above. There were 75 districts in the 14 zones of Nepal, and each had a representative in the Rastriya Panchayat. The 15 districts with a population of more than 100,000 were assigned one additional member each, making a total of 90. Fifteen members of the Rastriya Panchayat were elected by the officially recognized and controlled class, organizations, four each by the Peasants' Organization and the Youth Organization, three by the Women's Organization and two each by the Ex-Servicemen's Organization and the Labour or the Workers' Organization. The remaining four members of the 109 elected members of the Rastriya Panchayat came from the Graduates' Constituency.

The 90 Rastriya Panchayat members elected through the Zonal Assemblies (Anchal Sabhas) were directly elected by a simple majority ranging from 46 votes (in the case of the Mahakali and Karnali zones) to 98 votes (in the case of the Bagmati zone). Further, the electoral regulation provided that candidates for membership in the Rastriya Panchayat had to be members of the 11-member District Panchayat in the district where the Rastriya Panchayat seat was being contested. The candidates' proposer and seconder also had to be among the 11 members of that particular District Panchayat. These restrictions limited the choice of candidates for membership of the Rastriya Panchayat to a maximum number of two to three from any particular district. What was worse was that, in that situation, it was possible for a candidate to get himself elected to the national legislature if he could win over to his side eight out of the eleven members of the Panchayat of the district from which he was seeking election despite an almost complete lack of popular support in that district. Even the Rastriya Panchayat members who had actually contested elections through Zonal Assemblies were directly elected by an average of less than thirty votes. To put it in another way, ninety members of the Rastriya Panchayat were, even theoretically speaking, directly elected only by a fraction of a total number of 1,018 voters. The electoral arrangement which made the Zonal Assembly elect members from each of its districts to the Rastriya Panchayat also made it possible for a member with very little support in his own district to represent it in the national legislature. If he could secure a proposer and a seconder from his own District Panchayat, he could get himself elected with the support of a majority of members of District Panchayats other than his own. This method of election was undemocratic since the candidate elected as a representative of a particular district did not always prossess a representative character. Further, the procedure for election discriminated against the people of the Tarai area in two ways: first, by allowing the Tarai districts with a much larger population the same voting strength as that of the hill districts, and secondly, by making it impossible for the Tarai candidates to be elected to the Rastriya

Panchayat from his own district without the support of the members of the hill District Panchayats in that zone.

The representatives of the class organizations in the Rastriya Panchayat were for some time elected on the basis of Preferential Proportional Representation by the total strength of the Central Committee of these organizations, which, in each case, did not exceed 150 members. After 1972, the electoral colleges for election of members to the Rastriya Panchayat from class organizations were expanded to include members of the working committee of all districts. Chairmen of all the Anchal (Zonal) Assemblies, the members of the Central Working Committee and the sitting members of the Rastriya Panchayat from class organizations. But, even then, the total number of voters in the cast of the class organizations in the latest election was increased to only 861 in the case of the Peasants' Organization, 860 in the case of the Women's Organization, 861 in the case of the Youth Organization, 697 in the case of the Labour Organization and 569 in the case of the Ex-Servicemen's Organization.

Despite the limited nature of the franchise, the Graduates' Constituency, composed of about 13,000 college graduates in the country, had proved to be the most representative of all constituencies under the Panchayat system. All registered graduates in the country elected directly from among themselves four members to the Rastriya Panchayat on the basis of Preferential Proportional Representation, and every college graduate could freely contest the election from this nation-wide constituency.

The Graduates' Constituency

Of the 22 candidates for the four graduates' seats in the 1971 elections, 17 agreed to run on a common platform that advocated several major changes in the existing political system: (1) that elections to the national legislature should be direct and based on the principle of universal adult suffrage; (2) that the Prime Minister be appointed by the King on the recommendation of the legislature; (3) that all restrictions on fundamental rights be removed; and (4) that the sessions of the legislature be made open to the public. There was nothing particularly new in this platform since many members of the Rastriya Panchayat, including all members elected from the Graduates' Constituency in 1967, had voiced similar demands previously. What was new was Prime Minister Kirtinidhi Bista's response. He denounced the 17 candidates of opponents of the Panchayat system and sought to mobilize the electorate against them through the government-controlled press and radio, and by a circular to all government employees instructing them to support his own four-man panel of candidates. Bista suffered an embarrassing setback when his candidates had run on the four-point 'opposition' platform. The regime's response to the demands of the most enlightened section of the society has been, to put it mildly, negative.

Even more embarrassing to the government was the spotlight placed upon the candidacy of Ramraja Prasad Singh, a young Supreme Court lawyer, who was the only candidate to advocate directly an immediate return to 'the golden ear of parliamentary rule'—and thus, implicitly, the abolition of the Panchayat system. His victory in the election, while no immediate threat to the regime, was a moral defect for the government and a clear indication of the overwhelming support for parliamentary democracy among the educated elite in the country. The sense of uncertainty in the government was indicated by the series of events that followed: the reluctance of the presiding officer of the Rastriya Panchayat to swear-in Ramraja Prasad Singh along with the other newly-elected members; his arrest in the lobby of the legislature in a highly provocative manner by plainclothesmen; his trial and conviction by a special tribunal; his release from prison under royal amnesty, and finally his swearing-in by royal command as a member of the Rastriya Panchayat.

The story does not end there, however, as after his release Singh continued to advocate a return to parliamentary democracy at a series of public meetings in various parts of the country. He was finally rearrested in October 1971 and then expelled from the Rastriya Panchayat, allegedly for having violated the legislature's code of conduct. Singh's contribution had been to test the flexibility of the Panchayat system and determine whether the present constitutional system could be amended peacefully in response to popular demands. The conclusion to be drawn, obviously, was that it could not. This was further confirmed by the more than year-long imprisonment under the Security Act of two other members of the National Panchayat from the Graduates' Constituency, who had stood for the four point platform.

Direct elections for the Village (Gaun) and Town (Nagar) executive committee Panchayats, although held by show of hands initially in 1961-62, were later held by secret ballot. Until 1967, elections were conducted and supervised by the regular Zonal and District Officers of the government civil service, but the 1967 amendment to the constitution provided for an independent election commission to prepare electoral rolls and supervise the conduct of elections both for various Panchayat bodies and for the different offices of the class organizations at all levels. The capacity of the government to influence the outcome of elections through their officers of various levels did not decline at, because, in practice, the Election Commission had to seek the assistance of the regular government servants in its work.

Administrative Confusion

The confusion in the working of the Panchayat system was caused by an attempt to replace a 'political process' with a 'bureaucratic process' as though these processes were interchangeable. On the one hand, King Mahendra repeatedly emphasized in the text of the constitution and in his public pronouncement that decentralization was the most important feature of the Panchayat system. He did not, however, make it clear whether this would imply curtailment of his own royal powers in practice. On the other hand, there was a clear and unmistakable trend towards increasing centralization and concentration of all power in the hands of the King. The 1967 constitutional amendments provided for direct appointment by the King of the Anchaladhishes (Zonal Commissioner), Ambassadors and the Commander-in-Chief of the Nepal Army. The centralizing tendency was also manifest in the replacement of the former Zonal Panchayat by the Anchal Committee, which has the Anchaladhish as its Chairman and the elected Chairman of the representative Zonal Assembly as its Vice-Chairman. Again, at the level of district administration, the inherent conflict of powers and responsibilities continued as before between the Chairman and the Vice-Chairman of the District Panchayat along with its other members on the one hand and the government appointed Chief District Officer on the other, who was made to act as Executive Secretary to the District Panchayat. While the Chief District Officer was supposed to take orders from the elected office bearers of the District Panchayat, he was held responsible to the government in Kathmandu for the maintenance of law and order, and for the handling of other important affairs of the district. Later, apparently to solve the confusing lines of responsibility. the Chief District Officer was made to function independently of the District Panchayat as was the case before the arrangement was put into effect, and the Panchayat Development Officer took the place of the Chief District Officer as the government appointed Executive Secretary to the District Panchayat. But the old situation of conflict of powers and responsibilities between government officials and elected officials continued to plague district politics and administration.

The fact that the Zonal Commissioners were the King's political appointees while the Chief District Officer, like other District Officers, was a member of the regular civil service under various ministries of the government in Kathmandu, created practical difficulties in the evolution of satisfactory working relations between the two. The position of the Anchaladhish, the Zonal Commissioner, tended to be untenable because he had less administrative experience than regular civil servants at the district or zonal administration levels and also no local political influence comparable to that of the District Panchayat.

Thus, he was not in a position to command respect on his own by inspiring confidence either in the district and zonal level civil servants or in the district political elite. Whatever influence or standing he had was only because of his position as the King's direct appointee.

The most serious problem that confronted the Panchayat system in the field of political and administrative decentralization was that of revolving the inherent contradictions illustrated above.

Decentralization?

The new Panchayat system does not reflect any real decentralization or deconcentration of political and administrative power. As pointed out by Bhuwan Lal Joshi and Leo E. Rose, it is 'an attempt to rationalize the administrative process by creating viable institutions in areas where a serious lacuna had previously existed, thus providing the basis both for a modernized administrative system and for agencies through which economic development programmes could be implemented.

The Village Panchayats, the Town Panchayats and the District Panchayats have been given limited taxation and administrative powers. Their administrative functions include assisting development programmes, supervising and managing the village-, the district-, or the municipality-owned or controlled property, and maintaining certain records and statistics. The village Panchayats are granted judicial jurisdiction in minor civil and criminal cases. The claim that the new Panchayat system represents decentralization of political power and functions is completely invalid inasmuch as the central government's ultimately authority is maintained intact by granting the Panchayat Ministry discretionary power to suspend or dissolve a Panchayat and replace it with a provisional Panchayat authorized to exercise the same powers.

Zonal Committee

Until its abolition the Zonal Committee (Anchal Samiti), consisting of the office-bearers of various class organizations at the zonal level, had as its Chairman a Zonal Commissioner directly appointed by the King and as its Vice-Chairman the elected Chairman of the Zonal Assembly (Anchal Sabha). The 1967 amendment to the Constitution abolished the Zonal Panchayats in favour of the Zonal Committees. The Zonal Assembly, however, was retained as before merely as an electoral college to elect representatives to the Rastriya Panchayat from each of the districts in a particular zone.

Slight confusion has been caused by a misleading use of the 'Panchayat' nomenclature in relation to both the Panchayats at the various levels and the Zonal Committee on the one hand and the Rastriya Panchayat on the other. The Panchayats at the village and the district level, like the Zonal Committee, are smaller executive committees intedned for carrying on the administration of the village or the town or the district, whereas the Rastriya Panchayat is a national legislature and thus resembles the larger District or Zonal Assemblies or Sabhas in form and functions.

The Rastriya Panchayat

Although the Rastriya Panchayat had played a limited role in policy and decision-making on national issues and had served primarily as a rubber stamp for royal wishes, considerable political interest was centred on it. Frankly speaking, much of the activity and participation at the various levels of the Panchayat system and the class organizations seemed to be concerned merely with their character as means for election to the Rastriya Panchayat. The powers and privileges of the Rastriya Panchayat as outlined in the 1962 Constitution resemble those of Sallabkar Sabha, the Advisory Assembly under the Advisory Assembly Act of 1952 more closely than those of the parliament under the 1959 Constitution. This was true notwithstanding the fact that, unlike the old Advisory Assembly, the Rastriya Panchayat had mandatory powers in certain areas.

The Rastriya Panchayat could discuss any matter other than the conduct of the members of the royal family and the measures taken by judges in the exercise of their reponsibilities. Laws could be passed without the approval of the Rastriya Panchayat, but royal assent had to be obtained at the final stage. The basic procedure was the same as in the 1959 parliamentary constitution. There was, however, a remarkable difference in the approach and attitude towards legislation. Although royal assent to laws passed by parliament was taken for granted under the 1959 Constitution, a more active role was visualized for the King in the legislative process in the post 1960 era, since he was the real head of the executive departments of the government under the new system. The King had a real and wide veto power which in the last resort could not be challenged or overruled by the Rastriya Panchayat.

Furthermore, the King could require the legislature to 'submit its opinion' before the passage of any bill which was under consideration. The King could consider such opinion and after that, give assent to the bill either in the form in which it was presented to the 'Rastriya Panchayat or as altered'. Although the so-called principle of royal initiative was observed with 'money' or financial bills, and bills relating to the subject of defence in parliament under the 1959 Constitution, the Constitution did not require the cabinet to obtain prior consent of the King to initiate these bills. The 1962 Constitution made specific provisions in these matters.

The Council of Ministers

The relationship between the Rastriya Panchayat and the Council of Ministers was not clearly defined in the 1962 Constitution. While the Rastriya Panchayat apparently had some powers of control over Ministers, the Ministers could not be said to be entirely subject to the restrictions implied by the constitutional provisions. Ministers, however, had to be appointed from among the members of the Rastriya Panchayat and if non-members were appointed they had to be elected to that body within six months of their appointment. The King appointed the Ministers, and there is nothing in the Constitution which required him to consult the legislature in making them.

Even the 1967 amendment to the Constitution merely indicated that, if the King wished, he might consult the legislature in appointing the Prime Minister in a manner to be determined by him. The King's choice of Ministers was not limited in practice even by the constitutional provision that required Ministers to be members of the Rastriya Panchayat, since a fixed percentage of the membership of the legislature was composed of the King's own nominees.

Furthermore, once a Minister was appointed, the Rastriya Panchayat had only limited control over him. Even the passage of a no-confidence motion by a two-thirds majority of the total membership of the Rastriya Panchayat would not lead to a Minister's dismissal, since the Constitution left the final decision to the King. Thus the principle of ministerial responsibility which animated the 1959 Constitution was modified by the 1962 Constitution to permit the King to dismiss or retain a Minister without reference to the support he enjoyed in the Rastriya Panchayat.

Royal Prerogatives

The provisions of the 1962 Constitution show a considerable expansion of royal prerogatives compared to those contained in the Constitution. This was apparent, as has been pointed out, in respect of the relationship of the Crown with the Council of Ministers and the legislature, and also in respect of the wide 'emergency' and discretionary powers assumed by the King. According to Article 81 of the Constitution of Nepal, if His Majesty is of the opinion that a grave emergency exists whereby the security of the whole of Nepal or any part thereof is threatened by war, external aggression or internal disturbance, His Majesty by proclamation may suspend any of the Articles of the Constitution indefinitely until such time as His Majesty is satisfied that grave emergency no longer exists. The emergency powers of the King cover a very wide range, and the perfunctory legal restrictions placed on them are apt to be ineffectual, thereby leaving the King free to suspend, amend and abrogate the 1962 Constitution as easily or lightly as the 1959 Constitution. The 1962 Constitution has already been amended twice in 1967, and in 1975, every time centralizing increased authority in the King.

An example of the use of the Royal Prerogative concerns the selection of Ministers and Prime Ministers. The key ministers had usually been selected from the ranks of the nominated members to the Rastriya Panchayat and had been given important portfolios. After the 1963 elections, a nominated member became the Chairman of the Council of Ministers and also the Prime Minister for sometime. Four out of a total of five Prime Ministers during the last 12 years of the Panchayat era have been the incumbent Ministers, 'returned unopposed' to the National Assembly from their constituencies. Of the three Prime Ministers appointed during King Birendra's first four years' rule, the last did not even belong to the assembly before he was appointed Prime Minister. Critics have regarded this as a deliberate attempt on the part of the King to downgrade not only the office of Prime Minister but also the Rastriya Panchayat itself by making clear its subordinate position in the new political set-up.

The 1967 amendment to the Constitution limited the tenure of office of the Prime Minister to a maximum period of five years, although no Prime Minister has been elected or appointed in consultation with the Rastriya Panchayat up to now. Since the emergence of strong men such as Bhimsen Thapa and Jang Bahadur Rana as Prime Ministers historically always presaged a decline in the royal powers, King Mahendra sought to prevent the growth of strong popular figures by restricting the term of elected Prime Ministers to a maximum period of five years.

On the other hand, King Mahendra frequently used the Rastriya Panchayat to serve his personal and propaganda interests by referring to it as the highest legislative body representative of the people of Nepal. For example, on the eve of his second State visit to the United States in the autumn of 1967, King Mahendra, in an effort to cement the nation's view on the desirability and effectiveness of the Panchayat system, persuaded the Rastriya Panchayat to endorse unanimously his own suggestion that the Panchayat system had become an integral part of the life of the people of Nepal and admitted of no alternative. Some of the members of the Rastriya Panchayat suggested in a guarded manner that it was not entirely up to them to give such a verdict, and that it should be better if a popular referendum were organized on the question. But no attention was paid to this suggestion.

Perhaps the King's attitude towards political parties and organizations as manifested by the 1967 amendment to the Constitution reflects the spirit of the Panchayat system more than anything else in the Constitution. The 1962 Constitution was faithfully silent on the question of political parties, which were banned in practice merely by the Royal Ordinance of 15 December, 1960. This later acquired the form of a law called the Control of Organizations and Associations Act.

Theoretically, the Constitution permitted parties, because it is an accepted principle of jurisprudence that what the law does not expressly forbid it permits. However, the 1967 Amendment to the Constitution, while granting the right to freedom of association, expressly forbade the political parties and such organizations as were motivated by political considerations. Thus a ban on political parties and organizations was introduced as a basic and permanent feature of the Panchayat system. Since no form of political alignment on the basis of certain agreed principles or details of programme is permitted even inside the Rastriya Panchayat, the effectiveness of the Rastriya Panchayat as a representative institution and legislative body has been seriously compromised.

Zone of Peace

Nepal's commitment to peace and its geopolitical situation have led it to desire to be declared a Zone of Peace. The objective of the foreign policy of the Panchayat System, is to endeavour to make Nepala a Zone of Peace by adhering to the basic values of the United Nations and the principles of non-alignment.

Nepal's Peace-Zone objectives are incorporated in the Constitution of the country.

The country has undertaken to abide by a seven-point obligation provided that those supporting the Zone of Peace proposal do so on a reciprocal basis.

The seven points are:

(a) 'Nepal will adhere to the policy of peace, non-alignment and peaceful co-existence and will constantly endeavour to develop friendly relations with all countries of the world, regardless of their social and political systems and, particularly with its neighbours on the basis of equality and respect for each other's independence and sovereignty.

(b) Nepal will not resort to the use of threat or force in any way which might endanger peace and security of other countries.

(c) Nepal will seek peaceful settlement of all disputes between itself and other state or states.

(d) Nepal will not interfere in the affairs of other states.

(e) Nepal will not permit any activity on its soil that is hostile to other states supporting this proposal and, in reciprocity, the states supporting this proposal will not permit any activities hostile to Nepal.

(f) Nepal will continue to honour the obligations of all the existing treaties which it has concluded with other countries as long as they remain valid.

(g) In conformity with its policy of peace and non-alignment, Nepal will not enter into any military alliance nor will it allow the establishment of any foregn military base on its soil. In reciprocity, other countries will not allow establishment of military bases on their soil directed against Nepal.'

Objectives

The objectives of the Panchayat polity are to preserve national sovereignty and independence and create a developed, exploitation-free democratic society. These objectives can be categorized under three specific headings.

Political

The Panchayat System will continue to nourish and sustain nationalism for the preservation of national independence under the leadership of the Crown.

Social

Emancipation of the Nepalese people from all kinds of social exploitations so as to make social justice available to all is one of the objectives of the Panchayat System.

In Nepalese society social evils such as, polygamy, child-marriage, casteism and untouchability were rampant because of illiteracy and superstition. Aware of the need for eradicating them, the Panchayat system has introduced several measures to ameliorate the situation. The amendment to the *Mulki Ain*—the Law of the Land—with provision of ending the traditional caste system is an important measure taken in this respect.

Economic

Panchayat, since its inception has been striving to accelerate the pace of development to eliminate economic injustices. In the past decades some very important measures including the Land Reform Programme, have been undertaken to improve the quality of life of the people, that of those below the poverty line, in particular. The Basic Needs Programme adopted by the country to enable the people to meet their minimum requirements in the six areas of food, clothing, housing, health service, education and security by the turn of the century in 2000 A.D. shows the national commitment. The Panchayat System will further accelerate the process of economic development to raise the quality of life of the people.

Structure and Governance

Elections

Structurally the Panchayat System extends from the Village or Town to the national legislature. A number of Panchayat bodies—the Village or Town Assembly, Village or Town Panchayat, District Assembly, District Panchayat and Zonal Assembly—each linked with the other function as parts of the larger whole, the structure of the Panchayat System of the country.

Elections to the unicameral National Panchayat is held through secret ballot on the basis of adult franchise for a period of five years. Any member of the national legislature can be a candidate for the office of the Prime Minister and one who succeeds in obtaining 60 per cent votes of the total membership of the House is recommended for the Prime Minister's Office. Thus the Prime Minister is appointed by the King at the recommendation of the legislature. The Council of Ministers is responsible to the National Panchayat and ministers are collectively as well as individually accountable for the conduct of their official responsibilities.

The presiding officers of the National Panchayat—the Chairman and the Vice-Chairman—are elected by at least 60 per cent of the total membership of the national legislature and then appointed by the King.

The national legislature has Committee system to facilitate its functioning. The Steering Committee advises the Chairman on conducting the business of the House. There are six other Committees:

1. The Panchayat Committee,
2. The Finance Committee,

3. The Social Committee,
4. The Water Resources Committee,
5. The Public Accounts Committee, and
6. The Development Committee.

These committees function within their respective spheres.

Members of the Village Assembly and Town Assembly responsible for analysing and evaluating the work of the Village Panchayat and Town Panchayat are directly elected through secret ballot on the basis of adult franchise.

The Village Panchayat, the executive body of the Village Assembly and the grassroot political unit of the System, is entrusted with the responsibility of carrying out development activities and adjudiciaral of all local disputes. Its members including the Pradhan Pancha and Upa-Pradhan Pancha (the Chief and the Deputy Chief) are directly elected. The members including the Pradhan Pancha and Upa-Pradhan Pancha of the Town Panchayat are also elected through secret ballot on the basis of adult franchise.

Fundamental Rights

The Panchayat System is responsive to the socio-political needs of the people. The Constitution guarantees the fundamental rights of the people for development of their personality, security of life, liberty and property. The basic rights such as the right to equality before law, right to freedom of speech and expression and freedom of movement in any part of the country, right to property, and the right to constitutional remedy are incorporated in the Constitution to give substance to the Panchayat System's democratic ideas.

The independent judiciary set up under the provision of the Constitution is responsible for protecting the rights of people against any encroachment.

Synthesis

The Panchayat System, as the mainstream of national life,

is founded on popular consent. Equipped with powerful democratic instruments of secret ballot and adult franchise, effective participation of people at different levels under the Decentralisation of Authority programme, the Nepalese people are engaged in creating a just, exploitation-free, democratic society. The 60.32 per cent turnout of voters in the last general elections to the national legislature in 1986 indicates popular participation and support.

Structure of the Panchayat Polity

THE CROWN

Prime Minister and Council of Ministers	*Chairman and Vice-Chairman*
The Prime Minister elected from among the members of the national legislature is appointed by the King and his ministry.	The Chairman and the Vice-Chairman are elected from among the members of the national legislature and the appointed by the King.

National Panchayat

Parliament

140 members of the National Panchayat, 112 are members from different districts through secret ballots on the basis of adult franchise and 28 members from different walks of life are appointed by the King.

Zonal Assembly

District Panchayat office-bearers and members are ex-officio members of the Zonal Assembly.

|

District Panchayat

District Assembly

The District Panchayat office-bearers and members are elected for five years by the Village or Town Assembly members.

The Village or Town Panchayat office-bearers are members of the District Assembly.

|

Village and Town Panchayat

Village and Town Assembly

The Village/Town Panchayat is composed of chairman of the nine wards and pradhan and up-pradhan panch of the Village/ Town Panchayat.

Members and office-bearers of the Village or Town Assembly are elected for five years through secret ballots on the basis of adult franchise.

|

Electorate

The Dominant King

However, on another occasion, the King did officially respond to a joint petition sent to him by 64 members of the Rastriya Panchayat. This occurred following the arrest of a member under the Preventive Detention Act on 10 July, 1967, when the budget session of the Rastriya Panchayat was in progress. In the King's reply to this joint petition, communicated to all the members of the Rastriya Panchayat, the complaints of the members against the high handedness and arbitrary acts of the ministers were lightly dismissed. In addition, the petitioners were asked threateningly whether the very act of their collective sponsorship and signature of a petition was not prompted by a spirit of factionalism. The King's communication, although meant only for members of the Rastriya Panchayat and described as secret by the Rastriya Panchayat Chairman, meanwhile gained wide currency and became the subject of conversation among many of the politically conscious people of Nepal.

Incidents such as this make it quite clear that the future of the Panchayat system in Nepal depends on its flexibility and capacity to accommodate the many diverse political and economic forces that will inevitably be released by the process of modernization. The real test of the 1962 Constitution is whether it will succeed in containing and satisfying popular demands for reforms when they arise. King Mahendra thought that political parties by their very nature were factional bodies and hence disruptive of national unity. He created the machinery for implementation of his 'Back to the Village' programme, and also the class organizations as a substitute for political parties in an attempt to mobilize popular energy and direct it along nationally profitable channels. Time alone will show whether these efforts have fostered national unity or national frustration. For the present, it has been even the official view that the class organizations and the 'Back to the Village' National Campaign have not been very effective in fulfilling their projected goals.

'Class' Organizations

The so-called class and professional organizations are obviously not based on economic classes. They were created to denounce the concept of class-conflict in favour of a kind of class-coordination which is the real motivation behind the Panchayat system. Before 1960 organizations similar to the present class organizations functioned, but merely as affiliations of the political parties. They did not have the same important role envisaged for them in the present Panchayat system. The class organizations now enjoy a sort of organizational monopoly in their respective spheres, since parallel unofficial organizations are not permitted by government regulations.

A number of students' organizations and women's organizations were forced to dissolve before the class and professional organizations of peasants, youth, labourers, women, students, children and ex-servicemen were set up in 1961. The new organizations were formed under the direct sponsorship and supervision of a government ministry, the National Guidance Ministry. Although the professed object at the beginning was to grant full autonomy to these organizations and leave them free of government control if and when they had grown up to their sense of responsibility, such autonomy was never in fact encouraged. Indeed, the government managed to increase rather than lessen its control over them after the National Guidance Ministry itself was dissolved. The class organizations in Nepal are not 'representative' but are 'client-oriented', the client being the government. As a matter of fact the members of the class organizations are not active at all and have not been able to develop even the subject-participant orientation which characterizes the political culture of states where a single party dominates the system.

The students' agitation from 1963 to 1965 for free students' unions in colleges and in the Tribhuvan University forced the government to dissolve the government-sponsored students' organizations which the overwhelming majority of students had had nothing to do with ever since their inception. The 1967 amendment to the Control of Organizations Act prohibited not only politically motivated organizations of every kind but also demands or agitation for them in any form.

The 'Back to the Village' National Campaign

The 'Back to the Village' National Campaign was launched by the late King Mahendra through a message to the Rastriya Panchayat, Nepal's national legislature, in 1967. The message along with the programme of the campaign was published in a booklet under a red cover with a blue border, which had a striking resemblance to Chairman Mao Tse-tung's little red book. And also displayed prominently, perhaps as a conspicuous proof of Nepal's non-alignment, on a single page in that booklet itself, was a quotation from King Mahendra which was in fact merely a literal Nepali adaptation of the late American President

John F. Kennedy's famous sentence: 'And so, my fellow Americans: ask not what your country can do for you—ask what you can do for your country.'

The following ten items are listed as the main planks of the programme for the Back to the Village National Campaign: (1) to strengthen and develop the feeling of nationalism and national unity, (2) to explain the importance of partyless Panchayat democracy which admits of no alternative, and to strengthen the partyless spirit, (3) to make one's conduct and behaviour conform to the country's non-aligned foreign policy, (4) to start a campaign with a view to ending corruption, injustice, oppression and unnecessary delay because of a 'red-tapes' mentality, (5) to create a sense of consciousness and dynamism among members of the rural community, (6) to help successfully implement the on-going programmes of land reform, reform of the legal code, social reforms and national reconstruction, (7) to promote the growth of the cooperative spirit and to propagate and develop cooperative (Sajha) programmes, (8) to explain to the people the importance of aforestation and the protection of flora and fauna, (9) to stress the value of the growth of agricultural production, and (10) to arouse on a nationwide scale consciousness of need to encourage and expand handicrafts and cottage industries suited to local needs.

Apart from some official enthusiasm initially shown in the implementation of the programme, the people were never enthusiastic about the Back to the Village Campaign, and because of the absence of trained and dedicated cadres, the campaign was altogether lacking in sustained drive. The ideals of voluntary service and simple and austere living could not be inculcated in the minds of the people merely through official propaganda. The life and conduct of those sitting in high places fell far too short of showing exemplary behaviour to the people. Hence the failure of the Back to the Village National Campaign even in emphasizing the value of manual labour and of conveying the message to the people that work is worthwhile.

The 1973 edition of the Back to the Village National Campaign booklet contains the latest amendments to its programme and work procedures and the scheme for the evaluation of the workers of the Panchayat system along with a message from King Birendra. The message seeks to highlight development as the object of politics and also emphasizes the moral obligation on the part of Panchayat political workers to regard service of the people as the means of gaining popular trust and of rising to a higher position in the political hierarchy. While emphasizing the value of the Back to the Village National Campaign to the people of Nepal who live mostly in villages, the King has reaffirmed his belief in the campaign as the precursor of a society without exploitation, which is the proclaimed goal of the Panchayat system.

The Panchayat System under King Birendra

King Birendra Bir Bikram Shah Dev, who succeeded his father in January 1972, has introduced certain basic or substantive changes in the Panchayat system. In his initial public statements immediately following his accession to the throne, he occasionally hinted that the Panchayat system afforded scope certain changes in accordance with the spirit of the times. But his attitude on the question of allowing or initiating changes in the Panchayat Constitution seemed to grow rather rigid as has been evidenced by his more than year-long detention, under the Security Act, of former Prime Minister Surya Bahadur Thapa together with three other members of the Rastriya Panchayat. All four were arrested during the 1972-73 budget session of the Rastriya Panchayat after they had demanded at an open-air public meeting broadbased elections to the Rastriya Panchayat, the opening of its sessions to the press and public and a wider measure of fundamental rights. Their characterization of the present regime as a dual government of the Central Secretariat plus the Investigation and Enquiry Centre, was said to have been, more than anything else, the reason for their imprisonment.

King Birendra's plea for politics, strongly oriented towards development, initially manifested itself in the setting up of the National Development Council on 13 April, 1972, and in an amendment to the origins Back to the Village programme in 1973.

National Development Council

The National Development Council is not based on an act of the Rastriya Panchayat nor is it derived from an ordinance subsequently approved and formalized by the national legislature as a law. It was brought into existence by a royal decree issued through the Palace Secretriat.

According to Gorkhapatra, 15 September, 1976, King Birendra recognized the NDC, which had been formed on 9 June, 1972, under his own chairmanship. When the King remaining as Chairman, the Council now comprises all cabinet ministers; the chairman of the national assembly (Rastriya Panchayat), the standing committee of the King's Council or the Council of State (Raj Sabha), and the Central Committee of the Back to the Village National Campaign; three to five persons designated by His Majesty from among former Prime Ministers and the Chairman of the Council of Ministers; chairman of the committee of the national assembly (Rastriya Panchayat), members of the National Planning Commission, the Vice-Chancellor of the Tribhuvan University, the Governor of the State (Rastra) Bank of Nepal, the chairmen of the twenty-five district executive committees (Zila Panchayats). These are to be chosen by rotation for one year each, in such a manner that the fourteen zones, the Tarai, hill and inaccessible regions, are equitably represented, as also the chairman of the federation of chambers of commerce and industry, and three to five members who have gained reputations in different fields. It is further provided that each quadrennial session shall be attended by the chairmen of all the seventy-five district executive committees (Zilla Panchayats) by rotation.

The Council's first meeting from 26 to 28 February, 1973 was presided over by King Birendra himself. The meeting reviewed the mid-term progress of the Fourth Plan (1970-75) and examined the basic principles underlying the Fifth Plan.

The second meeting of the Council, which was held in Kathmandu from 24 to 26 September, 1973, examined the progress reports of various ministries for the fiscal year 1972-73 in the light of the Planning Commission's reaction. In addition, the ministers were called upon to answer questions regarding errors of omission and commission for which their respective departments were responsible. At the end of the second meeting King Birendra as President announced the setting up of two subcommittees to give final shape to the recommendations contained in the working papers prepared by the National Planning Commission. The first committee was to implement the establishment of a Development Pioneer Corps which would station in each of the four Regional Development Centres a 150 to 200 man pool of high-level, middle-level and low-level experts and technicians. The second committee was to implement the expansion of the Sajha (cooperative) sector of the economy. Further, the King asked the Evaluation and Recommendation Subcommittee to study whether changes in the targets of the plan were necessary in view of the experience acquired so far from its implementation. He also authorized the Evaluation and Recommendation Subcommittee to investigate the idea of a system of rewards and punishments for higher echelon officers in their work in implementing the plan.

The National Development Council and Rastriya Panchayat

The working relationship within the operational framework of the Panchayat system between the National Development Council, an extra-constitutional body, and the Rastriya Panchayat, Nepal's parliament, has implications for the evolution of the Panchayat system in the future and is, therefore, of considerable interest to a student of comparative politics. As the National Development Council seems to have the full backing of the King and also consists of a cross-section of the membership of the National Panchayat itself and other Panchayat bodies, there seems to be no visible sign of tension between the Rastriya Panchayat and the National Development Council. But it will be interesting to see whether the Rastriya Panchayat, when and if it comes into its own as a national legislature in the real sense, will allow its rightful role in economic development to be transferred to an extra-constitutional body such as the National Development Council as a Development Parliament.

In his introductory statement at the opening of the second meeting of the National Development Council, Dr Harka Bahadur Gurung, then Vice-Chairman of the National Planning Commission, rightly pointed out that 'it was the responsibility of the political units at the national level to reflect the people's aspirations in the formulation of development policies. However, whether or how far the existing political units at the national level may be able to represent popular aspiration is a different matter. In the course of his remarks, Dr Gurung added that 'if everyone engaged in the task of preparing development plans could be given clear instructions and directions by these units, it would go a long way in making the Fifth Five Year Plan more people-oriented'. This is indeed a very big 'if', in view of the fact that the general calibre and intelligence level of the personnel of the political units at the national level, not to mention the method of their election, would not seem to equip them for giving clear and precise instruction to the framers of the plan.

Regional Development Centres

King Birendra has sought to forge his own instruments to accelerate the pace of development on which he has laid great stress ever since becoming King. The National Development Council is the primary body the King intends to employ for development purposes. This Council has already acquired considerable prestige because of the King's personal and direct association with it as Chairman. It appears that the National Development Council will eventually have important ramifications throughout the country. Considerable stress has been laid on regional development, and the country has been divided into four development regions—the eastern, the central the western and the far-western development region. Four regional development centres have also been set up at Dhankuta, Kathmandu, Pokhara and Surkhet.

King Mahendra had originally planned to use the delecte District Panchayats and the Rastriya Panchayat as media for developmental purposes. When he was not satisfied with their role in promoting development the King then thought of another device, namely, a Zonal Committee consisting of a few nominees from the District Panchayats with the Zonal Officer or Anchaladhish as Chairman and the elected Chairman of the Zonal Assembly as Vice-Chairman. The Zonal Committee merits comparison with the National Development Council in one substantive respect. Both of these bodies are based on a combination of the principle of election with that of nomination. King Birendra is seeking to apply these principles on a wider scale, and it is perhaps too early to predict the results. However, it would seem that there is eventually bound to be an overlapping and duplication of jurisdiction and functions between the various hierarchies of the Panchayat organization and those of the National Development Council at all levels, unless something is done to define and demarcate their respective functions and jurisdiction clearly and in precise terms.

THE CROWN

To dwell on the Panchayat philosophy alone without reference to the Crown, the founder of the Panchayat political philosophy, will remain incomplete. The history of the Nepalese Crown is the longest in the history of monarchy in the world. It has, in its long and continuous history, been offering active leadership to the country and the people. The history of leadership by the Crown for the rights of the people is original speciality of the Nepalese monarchy. It is for this reason that the Nepalese Crown, the founder of the Panchayat democratic system, cannot, in fact, be put to comparision with the other monarchies of the world. In the history of all the Crowns in the world, the Nepalese Crown has appeared to be the most progressive.

Even in this twentieth century, the Crown in England, is a symbol of government by the people. The monarch in that country has proved out-and-out helpful in making the democratic system powerful. But in Nepal where democratic leadership has been obtained from the King himself, the Crown has been not only aidant to it but also its founder, protector and guide.

The Crown being so great and important in Nepal, the Nepalese politics and constitution mobilise themselves on the basis of the Crown. As the British system accepts the Crown as its central and co-ordinative power, so they have the Crown as their central power, and the main source and basis of nationality. So, in Nepal, no politics of whatever kind, not mobilishing itself on the Crown, can ever lead itself into the heart of the people.

Even the Rana rulers appeared to have well understood this truth about the Crown. In 1950, after His Late Majesty, King Tribhuvan, had with the royal family, left the palace and taken refuge in the Indian Embassy, they seated Prince Gyanendra, a child of three, on the throne and proclaimed him king. When they could depose King Tribhuvan and proclaim Prince Gyanendra king, they could rule the country even without a king, but they did not keep the country without a king. From this one may infer what great importance the Crown commands in Nepal. Even the absolute Ranarchy regarded the existence of the Crown as very essential and had not the courage to go to the extent of lessening its value.

In England, the continuous evolution of the parliament had begun right in the Medieval times, and among the other reasons for this, the main reason was the system of having a firm monarchy. Even in to-day's democratic system of government, there it is the Crown that safeguards the constitution, as the Nepalese Crown which protects the Nepalese constitution and popular welfare. This comes to mean that in England the Crown functions as a jury contending between parties and manages national unity during times of national emergency or crisis. Bagehot has regarded the prestige of the Crown as a very important part of the British Constitution. In Nepal, the

Crown is not only the part of the Constitution but its centre and very soul and the Constitution moves around this centre.

The struggle between the king and feudalism is not a new thing in the history of the world. According to an Indian writer, who opines that in Nepal where the power of the people has supported the King, monarchy has developed as a progressive institution; if the king had not led the Revolution in 1950, much blood and tear would have been shed and the struggle would have continued for a much longer time. The leadership by the king checked all this. This has made the importance of monarchy still greater. Therefore, the Revolution of 1950, made the position of the King more influential. The people of other countries, perhaps, do not have the good fate to get kings like Tribhuvan and Mahendra who put their life and throne to risk for the cause of freedom of the people. The history of Nepal makes it clear that in Nepal real inspiration for nationality and of democratic power has been derived from the Crown.

Great geniuses propound new principles and influence to a large extent, the forms and order of historical events. It is known to all that Rousseau in France, Lenin in Russia and Mahatma Gandhi in India have, through the media of their respective philosophies, exercised their influence on the progress of history. In our Nepal, Mahendra, the King beloved of people, has made the Panchayat system a political philosophy and changed the direction of the progress of the Nepalese history to a new direction. The proclamation of Panchayat Constitution on the first of Baishak, 2018, has turned the confused political history to a new direction. It is a revolutionary change. It is for this reason that the Nepalese people have got King Mahendra not only as the leader of the nation but also as a great political thinker. This Panchayat system, set up by H.M. the King, has come to existence as the result of the history incident of the first of Poush, 2017. The political thinkers, therefore, have opined that political principles depend on real situations and that they flourish before but not after them. In fact, principles are formed on events and the former influence the latter. The situation, previous to the first of Poush and following that date, made the framing and proclamation of the new constitution inevitable.

In accordance with the modern democratic tradition, a constitution to determine the form of the government selected by the people and the relation between its various organs; and, with that constitution as the basis, the election of the representatives of the people is held and a government is organised. Such as constitution is in some states framed by constitutional assembly; *e.g.*, the Indian constitution, and in some others, they are unwritten; *e g.*, the British Constitution. The British Constitution has not been framed by a constitutional assembly, as has been the Indian Constitution. The American Constitution has been drawn up by a convention composed of men very conversant with practical politics and the Nepalese constitution by a constitution drafting committee.

If it should be said that only constitution framed by constitutional assembly composed of members elected by the people is democratic, then the British and American constitutions should be accounted undemocratic, for they have not been framed by any constitutional assembly. But any democrat in the world can not at all call them undemocratic. On the contrary any attempt, on his part, at calling them so, will testify to his pseudo-democratism derived in the emulation of those constitutions themselves. This makes it obvious that it seems more proper from, the political point of view to call a constitution democratic for the reason that it has in itself democratic elements and its spirit is democratic than to call it so because it has been framed by a constitutional assembly.

On Falgun I, 2015, His Majesty, the King, gave his Nepalese people the constitution of the Kingdom of Nepal, framed by the constitution drafting committee. At that time, the many political parties acknowledged the constitution as democratic and participated in the general election; and, fighting in the election held according to the dicta of the constitution. The Nepali Congress, having obtained a majority of ballots, had formed its government. Even after the failure of the parliamentary system, His Majesty the King got a constitution befitting the changed circumstance and the Panchayat system prepared by a constitution drafting committee and gave it to the people, and according to the democratic tradition the National Panchayat, the supreme popular representative institution of the country was formed. It is, thus, obvious that to develop and help forward the democratic tradition and system the King himself has taken the lead.

Previous to the year 2007, there was not at all any question of a constitution of the representatives of the people. In the year, 2004, during the rule of the Rana Prime-Minister Padma Shamshere, a constitution had been drawn up; but it was, however, kept subjected to deliberation and did not come to practice. In 2007, King Tribhuvan proclaimed a democratic system of government and announced the Nepal Interim Constitution according to which the country was to be governed until the time a constitution fitting in with the democratic system of government would be prepared. It is from this point that the constitutional development of the Kingdom of Nepal appears to have had its commencement. On the historic basis of the democratic system that came in after 2007, and against the background of initial experiment with the constitution of 2015, there came the constitution of 2019, which has led to the organization of a government on the Panchayat system. This constitution may be looked upon as a development of the 2015 constitution, for the constitution is dynamic and it should be capable of mobilising and changing itself according to circumstances that naturally tend to change. As a result of this dynamism, it recame into light the constitution of 2019. Closely following the trend and firm thought, enunciated in the constitution of 2015, and adopting itself to the new political environment.

In America, after the declaration of independence in 1777, the thirteen colonies together accepted the Articles of Confederation and all unitedly formed the United States of America. A congress was organised for conducting its affairs. This continental congress was but a natural offspring of the British parliamentary system. But since the administration of the states as defined in the constitution of this confederation did not prove effective and the necessity of a strong central authority was felt, the new principle of political organization—the federal system of government was adopted and in 1789 A.D. the new constitution was put in to practice. It is in this way that the federal form of government came into existence in America. The system of government of which the American people had twelve years experience was based on the British parliamentary system; but the adoption of the federal system was necessiated by the historical tradition and environment. This new federal constitution was founded on the principle which already lay deep rooted in the political consciousness of the people. The progressive spirit lying embodied in the constitution of the United States, by well be understood from this too that, by the end of a long period of about 175 years, the constitution of the United States has known so much of change by the judicial enterpretation that, even if the people who framed the constitution come back to-day, it would certainly be difficult to say whether they drew it up. A constitution is an experiential experiment. It is not proper to judge any constitution merely by its form and declare with strength that it is good or bad.

Although it cannot be said that critics did not comment even on the constitution of 2015, yet it may here be added that the leader of the party having majority in the parliament, the ex-Prime Minister Mr. B.P. Koirala, had asserted that was a definite constitution and upon it they were marching ahead on the path of democracy. But only after an experimental experiment of eighteen months, the parliamentary system as prescribed by the constitution proved deterimental. The constitution of India has invested as much authority in the Indian President as did the Weimar constitution invest in the German head of the state in 1919. But there is no instance where the President of India has transgressed the democratic limits; yet the world knows that Hitler, exercising the powers granted by the Weimar constitution, had become a sole dictator. The genuineness of a constitution is judged by the fundamental principles it has inscribed in their application and its consequences.

The real spirit of a constitution is more important than its form. The Indian constitution has invested boundless power in the President, the British constitution has entrusted all powers to the Crown, and the American constitution has handed all executive powers over to the President. But the spirits of these constitutions being democratic, no instance is available in the histories of India, Britain and the United States, in which the democratic limits have been stepped over and absolute dictatorship is established.

The spirit of the Nepalese Constitution of 2015 was also democratic. The chief elements of a democratic constitution are (a) the selection of the people's representation on the basis of adult franchise, (b) the running of the government of the country by the representatives elected by the people, (c) the integrity of the supreme court, and (d) the safeguard of the fundamental rights. All these four elements were there incorporated into the constitution of 2015. The constitution of 2019 was framed on these very basic elements. Had the constitution of 2015 not been there, that of 2019 would not have been born. In the constitution of 2019 also, democratic elements like the highest national institution formed of representatives elected by the people by exercising the adult franchise and the integrity of the supreme court are ensured. In it there were provisions for the guarantee of fundamental rights and the participation by the people in the government. Leading the people along the path of democracy by giving them such a democratic constitution the Nepalese Crown is a novelty in the history of monarchy in the world.

As a matter of fact, a constitution should make room for such a system in the country which is related to the mode of living or way of life of its inhabitants. It is not only our opinion held up unanimously by the modern political scholars; but a similar trend of thought had flourished in Greece many years ago. According to the Greek political thinkers, "A constitution is not only an order in the administrative ranks but also an order of life". It can, therefore, be asserted that the Panchayat system prosecuted by the new constitution of 2019 is one related to the mode of living of the Nepalese people. At this point, however, the following inspirative sentences of His Majesty King Mahendra, the founder of the Panchayat system are specially being reffered to:

"Nobody gets a democratic simply by resorting to the propaganda that he is a democrat. Democracy is not merely the name of a system of government: but it is a definite way of living." Thus, King Mahendra gave his people a democratic constitution, got an election held, according to its dictates, and instituted the National Panchayat. He has, in this way set himself forth to the Nepalese people as the founder and protector of democracy.

According to the statement in Chapter V, clause No. 20 Sub-clause No. 2, that "the sovereignty of Nepal is invested in the King, and the King is the source of all rights executive, legislative and judicial." It is the Crown that is the source of sovereignty. The Crown, therefore, is above the law.

In all democratic constitutions, the whole power is vested in the supreme ruler in accordance with the constitutional tradition concerning his prestige. As well in the Indian constitution providing for a parliamentary system of government, the office of the President is prestige. He is never responsible to the judiciary for any work done by him in the capacity of the President. It is in him that all executive powers of the federation are vested. He is the supreme commander of the army, navy and the air-force. He appoints the Prime-Minister.

The constitution of India endows the President with the emergency powers so exclusively that during the period of national emergency all the powers of the country come solely under him, enabling him thereby to suspend even the fuandmental rights guranteed to this citizens. Thus, in view of the emergency powers vested in the President, the constitution of India appears to have made him the absolute dictator of India.

The President of the United States of America is not a titular head of the state like the King of England or the President of France but a de facto ruler. According to the constitution, all executive powers are invested in him. The British constitution acknowledges the very Crown as the source of all sovereignty. It does so till now. The Crown itself is the central power of British system of government. The supreme executive powers are invested in the Crown itself. The Crown is also the fountain of honour and is still now considered the fountain of justice. It appoints the Prime-Minister too. To, say, seeing to all these alone that the King of England and the President of India and the U.S.A. are dictators is but a mistake from the political angle of vision. In fact, they are not despots practically.

In our Nepal, there has floated down to our age an ideal which acknowledges the Crown as progressive and beloved of people and the protector of popular well-being and part of divinity. (Some of our holy texts state that nobody can become king unless he has some part of lord Vishnu in him). The Crown, therefore, holds essentially the highest station and commands esteem not only in the constitution but also in the heart of every Nepali. Nepalese people on the whole have full faith in the Crown, which offered leadership in lifting Nepal and the Nepalese people at times of crisis, in bringing in democracy for the well being of the people and in protecting their prestige and honour, and which, by giving a democratic constitution worth time and popular will, moved ahead on the path of democracy and called for national constitution according to the demand of the age Despite his being above the law, the King has kept himself within the democratic traditions and limits.

The constitution is the supreme law of the state. No law is complete in and success by itself. It is but a direction. The law and the rules depend on the good sense, awakening and dutifulness on the part of the people. Likewise, the success of democratic constitution depends on the democratic sensibility and vigilance on the part of the people. In Nepal, the King, by giving a definite constitution, has magnified the way to the development of democracy and the construction of the country.

During the period of 104 years, when most of the countries of the world, making all round progress, attained the summit of prosperity. Nepal lay dormant under the away of a family actocracy lagged far behind other countries of the world in the general race for progress. It is of the Crown that Nepal in this circumstance had the lendership is required for rising above this narrow to the new democratic atmosphere it could exhilarate itself and move forward in the path of progress.

The great responsibility of crowning the new-born democracy with success fell upon the shoulders of King Mahendra, the monarch who loves his subjects as his own children. Without careing for regal pleasants and gratifications, he has been working with a true sense of this great responsibility. Worthy, farsighted and hard-working, he is not only the King but alse the national leader of the Nepalese people. After 2007, the meritorious leadership by King Mahendra lifted the tremulous political atmosphere of Napal—Nepal, everweighed by partly politics, suffering for want of a deserving leader of the people, and at a fix obout discovering a sight way to a desired kind of politics and political stability from several political crises and catastrophes and set it aright.

It is by the efforts of His Majesty King Mahendra, that the politics of Nepal, engulfed in the marsh of various "ism" and political parties, cropped up to democracy and development. The very apt leadership by King Mahendra taught the Nepalese people to rise above the narrow limits of individual and party and to look out with pervasive eyes of national welfare, a genuine of national oneness. It also changed the ideology of party-appendage into the genuine feeling of national oneness and common allegiance to the sovereign.

The King entrusted different political parties with the government of the country and thereby gave them opportunities to work for the cause of the motherland. But none of the party-governments could at all succeed in reflecting popular well-being and offering substantial leadership to the people. The becomes clear if we turn over the pages of the history of Nepal, after 2007. The experiential experimentation of this period proved it that the revolution of 2007 and the democratic systematization of thereafter could not beget any worthy leader of the people. At the same time, the political atmosphere of this period has made it doubtless clear to the world that in Nepal King Mahendra is the only national leader. Thus by the leadership of the Crown itself, Nepal's politics crossed over the critical situation. This has enhanced the importance and the populority of the Crown.

In Nepal, the history of monarchy has defined the Crown as the principal protector of national well-being. The Crown is the source of inspiration for national unity, and a symbol of national feeling and culture. After 2007, the statesmen of the world found that in Nepal the Crown is the fountain of modern democracy. Democracy came into Nepal by the combined efforts of the King and the people, inspired by the Crown; the Nepalese people got the constitution by the inspiration of the Crown; and according to the constitution, the supreme institution representing the entire population was organised and government by the representatives of the people was formed. Thus the monarch himself gave his people a democratic constitution and constitutionally formed a government by the representatives of the people is a new event in the history of the world.

King Mahendra, having entrusted the responsibility of the government of the country to the representatives of the people, after the general election of 2015, kept himself, according to the democratic tradition, a constitutional monarch. He never objected to any democratic work and any project drawn up for the well-being of the country by the elected government and that he granted full scope of independent working to the people—elected government is testified to by the history of the system of working under the parliamentary system of government. The

King assented to the bills, even though they were vehemently protested against by the members of the opposition parties but passed by a majority of the ruling party; and this he did strictly in accordance with the parliamentary tradition. Although, according to the clause No. 42. Sub-Clause 9 (i) and (2) of the constitution of 2015 he could send the notice to both houses of the parliament that "he had not given his assent to the bills sent in for the royal assent" or that "he had sent them back for further thinking or consideration" to that house of the parliament where it had its genesis. In India too each bill passed by both the houses of the parliament is sent constitutionally for the assent of the President. The President may assent to a bill or refuse to do so, or even send it back repeatedly to the parliament with his recommendation for amendment. Thus His Majesty had the democratic and constitutional power to assent to any bill passed by the parliament or to refuse to do so, or even peruse it and send it back to the parliament for reconsideration, but he neither refused to assent any bill passed and brought in for his assent by the parliament nor did he send it back for reconsideration. This is expression of his progressiveness, his love for the democratic tradition and his regard for the democratic spirit and, at the same time, a challenge to those who mistake the Crown for an impediment to the development of the democratic system.

After 2007, until the act up the people-elected government, the King could take all the governmental powers to himself; yet for the purpose that the cabinets then shauld represent the people as far as possible, he gave chances to almost all ranking parties and their leaders to work the governmental machinery in a democratic way. During this period of nearly eight years, no substantial progress could be achieved nor could any atmosphere befitting demòcracy could be created. Even after the disorganisation of the Nepali Congress, the King could run the government by himself; but until the organisation of the people-elected government, he formed a cabinet composed of the personalities taken up from the people themselves, thereby placing upon their shoulder the entire responsibility of running the government of the country in a democratic way. This is a brilliant example of His Majesty's faith in democracy.

In any country, the development of the practice of acknowledgeing a specific personality for the vestment in him of its sovereign power, has taken place alongside of the development of the human civilisation. There exists no difference of opinion regarding this practice. But political scholars differ on what its form should exactly be. To a great extent, in Britain (where they have the parliamentary democracy) sovereignty rests constitutionally with the Crown, in India with the President and in Nepal with the Crown. The President of India is, in fact, decoration in the constitution and a titular ruler; according to the parliamentary tradition, the cabinet itself is the ruler de facto. In Britain, the actual power is vested in the cabinet. The monarch plays no role in the politics of the state. But the history of Nepal shows this that in Nepal the very Crown has given guidance and offered leadership for the welfare of the country and the people. His late Majesty, King Tribhuvena, made more popular the beloved leadership of the Crown, the leadership steadily made and strengthened by the former beloved kings like Drabya Shah, Ram Shah and Prithivinarayana Shah. And now since His Majesty King Mahendra, has offered historic leadership of the people for the all-round development and prosperity of the people, the Nepalese monarchy has never remained inert like a constitutional monarchy but has always kept active despite its strict adherence to the constitution.

It may be deemed necessary to dwell here to some extent on the constitutional monarchy. Before the development of the modern democratic system took place, the theory of the divine right of kings was very popular. The powers of kings were unlimited. To rule the people was their right granted to them by God. So it was the duty of the people to obey kings. The people had no right to question or move against the rights of kings. The theory held good in Britain till the 16th and 17th centuries, and was strongly propounded by King James 1st and Robert Filmer. In France Bousset had propounded this theory in support of the absolutism of Louis. Though, during the Middle ages, the monarchical government was generally acknowledged the best government, yet the Medieval political thinkers like Marsiglio and Nicholas had hinted at the sovereignty of the people. The limited monarchy consisted of the popular sovereignty.

The commencement of the Renaissance and the Reformation mark the beginning of the modern age in the history of Europe. Consequently logic came to dominate popular belief. In these circumstances, political thinkers like Hobbes and Rousseau propounded the Social Contract Theory, of which the purpose was that the right to rule was granted to kings not by Gods but by the consent of the people. In this very theory, Hobbes and Locke in England and Bodin in France accepted monarchy on logical grounds. But the concept of the modern democracy was founded on the thought that kings were granted the right to rule by the consent of the people.

According to Hobbes, the people combined to create the Leviathan (a symbol of the big sovereign) and granted him all the natural rights. Since they could not take back what they had already surrendered, they did not enjoy the right to protest against the ruler. Hobbes, thus had endeavoured to support the absolute monarch. In the beginning of the Renaissance an Italian statesman, Machiavelli—a child of the Renaissance-supported momarchy by a strange means. According to him, religion and morality were the means to the achievement of the political objective. He thought that the means, however immoral it be at first, would certainly turn moral after the achievement of the objective; and that king was successful who could accomplish his task by having recourse to power and cunning. Although Machiavelli was censured for his aforesaid opinion about the conduct of kings, yet his approach was practical. Whatever it be, Machiavelli too wished unify Italy torn asunder on account of its innate weakness and want of coherence, and bring it under one government. He, therefore, thought that if a state in the face of a crisis, all its people should combine to protect it by all available means.

Machiavelli' thought clearly showed the reflextion of the real condition of Italy of his time.

Bodin, a political scholar of the 16th century France, had attempted at supporting monarchy by his own theory of sovereignty. According to him, every state has its sovereignty thing supreme and indivisible. Since sovereignty should lay in the hands of the king, the king is sovereign. A monarch vested with this sovereign power was necessary to any state. So the monarch is essential. It was Bodin who first of all put sovereignty into operation in 1576.

The history of monarchy in Nepal makes it obvious that the Nepalese monarch is not like the one preached by Machiavelli, nor is it similar to the one emphasised by Bodin, nor does it even bear resemblence to the one pointed out by Hobbes. The Nepalese monarchy therefore, is different from the monarchies in Europe. The age-old history of the Nepalese monarchy has pronounced it that in Nepal there never came any circumstance where the king should be assisted to continue his office by resorting to the support of monarchy, ror came there any condition in which the king should work for the safeguard of his kingship bringing religion and morality under the control of politics.

Before the modern democratic system originated as an important consequences of the Renaissance, the power of king was unlimited according to the divine right theory; and as this theory began to loose hold, a new idea began to take root. The idea brought out and defined certain powers of the people and put them forth as one that could not be overstepped by kings. Consequently monarchies in many states came to be limited. Kings could not work at their own sweet will; they should work keeping within certain limits and in accordance with certain systems prescribed by the constitutions and defined by the laws of the states. This very trend of thought is the theory of limited or constitutional monarchy. So in a monarchy, the administration of the state is carried on according to a definite system mentioned in the constitution. The theory of constitutional monarchy has come forth as an effective means of checking up the tyrannical absolutism of kings overlooking the welfare and wellbeing of their subjects. When we approach the question whether the Nepalese monarchy is constitutional or not, we should not only turn to the slogan of constitutional monarchy but find it essential to pay heed to the matter of fact. It is worth being especially mentioned here that throughout the one thousand year-old history of the Nepalese monarchy, except during the Ranaeclipse that occurred within this long period the Crown or king has been an earnest protector of the people,—active, vigilant, inspirative and unsurvingly watchful for the safeguard of their well—being. The history of monarchy in Nepal makes it obvious that the monarch here is "an active monarchy working for the good of the people". The Nepalese monarchy is, therefore, quite different from any other monarchy of the world. The following are the ideals of the monarchy in Nepal:

(*1*) *The Hindu Ideal*: According to the Hindu ideal, the king is the protector of his subjects. Though the saying that the king possesses part of divinity supports the diving right of the king, yet does not prove his absolutism. Even a modern democratic constitution invests in the head of the state unlimited powers and endeavours to call forth people's faith in and honour to him; for example, the constitution of India invests unlimited powers in the President and makes his office unlimitedly prestige. Like wise, divine right is granted to the king, the head of the state on religious and ethical grounds; but this is done only to make the office of the king unlimitedly prestige, not to prove his absolutism. In the days gone by there were no constitutions drafted by any particular committees or constitutional assemblies which aimed at limiting the powers of kings, yet the kings should govern their subjects, strictly in accordance with certain rules or regulations. These rules or regulations were collectively called '*Rajdharma*' or 'the duty of kings'. Religious and ethical bases are far better founded than the constitutional basis. It is true of human psychology Rajdharma was founded on a solid ground of religion and morality. This '*Rajdharma*' put limits to the powers of kings more strictly than any constitution does today. The Nepalese monarchy has, therefore, always been constitutional and protector of the people.

(2) *The Ideal of the Shah Dynasty*: The Shah dynasty occupies a very important place in the history of the Nepalese monarchy whice has till today been protecting the people. This very characteristic of the Nepalese monarchy makes it entirely different from any monarch of any other country.

(3) *National Tradition*: The Nepalese monarchy has on it lasting stamp of the national tradition, which makes it different from any monarchy in any other part of the world. It is on account of this national tradition that the history of the Nepalese monorchy is the longest in the history of monarchy in the world. Development and progress in Nepal have been possible only by the never weakened co-operation between the king and people. Alongside the Nepalese monarch has not only been the political leader but also a spiritual one.

In this way, in Nepal the very '*Rajdharma*' was the constitution which put limits to the powers of the king. Here monarchy never turned absolute. Any constitution to-day may be changed by the majority vote in a parliament or assembly composed of the representatives of the people; but the *Rajdharma*' could never be changed, for it was above all.

Therefore it can be said with certainty that the monarchy in Nepal reflects all the fore-going elements. So the Nepalese monarchy has a social-political and spiritual basis.

The Nepalese monarchy exhibits this modern trait that it is limited by an integration in it of the '*Rajdharma*' and the modern democratic constitution. According to the dictates of the '*Rajdharma*' no king, devoid of royal virtues, can claim the right of setting as a king; and in accordance with the democratic tradition, no king can even overlook the welfare of the people. Nepal today has got a king, who deserves holding the '*Rajdharma*' is endowed with all virtues, and shows affection on the people. This is the characteristic quality of the Nepalese monarchy, which has remained intact and unimpared right till now.

King Mahendra, the leader of the nation, has never transgressed the limits of the constitution which he personally gave to the people. Even the royal proclamation of Paush 1, 2017, did not violate the constitution that was accepted by the people and the political parties alike and on the basis of which the different parties contended in the election and got the parliament established. And the Nepali Congress, having won majority, organised its government. Therefore, that is the constitutional monarchy, in which the monarch functions, keeping within the limits of the constitution, the Nepalese monarchy is, for that reason, a "real active constitutional monarchy", which stands as a special trait in the national monarchical character of Nepal.

The history of Nepal has made the Nepalese Crown more impressive. Ever since the Panchayat system began under the leadership of the Crown, an unprecedented singularity has come to reflect itself on the politics of Nepal. The feeling of unity infused by the leadership of his His Majesty into the hearts of the people is a novelty in the history of Nepal. The people accorded, on a nation wide scale a unanimous support to the step of His Majesty, a support which none of the previous governments could obtain. This makes it evident that the people are and that the King is the pivot of the Nepalese politics. The destiny and existence of the Nepalese people is related to monarchy. This truth is the very soul of the Nepalese politics. To devaluate the Crown without any regard to this truth is to lack in farsightedness. And he who fails to understand this truth, fails to comprehend the politics of Nepal. In Britain, where they have a monarchical system similar to the one in Nepal, the people are not at all as much against monarchy as they are in the favour, so much so that the Labour Party there to-day, which vigouriously criticises the noble House of Lords, is not at all against monarchy. It does not, however, come to mean to any statesman that the people of Britain have no love for democracy. In the present century, when monarchy is taking its exit from the political stage of the world monarchy in England has won maximum popularity, while in Spain, a neighbour, monarch has come to an end. A distinguished political scholar of Britain Laski, has said that in Great Britain the monarchy is the symbol of democracy. The people of Britain won a big empire and created the best democratic atmosphere. There they could do by virtue of the Crown of their land. They discovered in the Crown the extraordinary glory and attraction, which not may be found in a President that is elected; and they saw an astounding unity under the leadership of the Crown in the days of national crisis.

Had the Crown not proved specially beneficial to them in fact, the progressive minded and democracy-loving people of Britain would certainly have done away with the institution of monarchy. The same people who disowned Henry VIII for the simple reason that he wedded a lady against the tradition of the soil, could certainly put an end to monarchy, too. They could easily set up republican form of government; they got at least two chances for that; one in 1649, when, after the beheading Charles first, Oliver Cromwell started the republic, and once again at the time when James II, having quarreled with the parliament, fled to France. But the republic could not continue for over twelve years, and even after James II had taken flight to France, the people of Britain insisted on monarchy itself and resumed owning monarchy by placing William of Orange and Mary, his wife, as joint sovereigns on the throne in 1689. This makes it evident, therefore, that the democratic people of Britain, because they had full faith in the special beneficiality of Kingship in their country, were not in favour of dispensing with it. This is, at the same time, a briliant example of the fact that monarchy is never hindrance to the development of democracy and that in any country only that institution which is desired and cherished by the people can thrive and develop on the people's good feeling for it. It is not only that the monarchy in Nepal is progressive, but also that the Nepalese politics, nationalism, culture and civilization are all reflected on the Crown, far more than on anything else.

The monarchy in Britain is founded on the support of popular will, while that in Nepal reflects the will and, at the same time, has been the founder of democracy and its guide. In many countries in the Medieval Europe, the rights of the people were restored through struggles against the divine rights of kings. In Britain too the right of the king had, after a long—time struggle, been diminished in a strange way so as to render it into means which could go helping alongside of the speed in the development of democracy. But in Nepal, since the King has been the protector of the popular well-being and guide, no conflict has ever been there between the King and the people. No part of the history of any other country will hardly have an instance where the king has taken the lead for the rights of the people. This is the characteristic quality of the Nepalese Crown. As a matter of fact, any political doctrine is a thought which is based on the feeling of the people. In Nepal, as in any other monarchical state, Kingship is a thought, which is so firmly founded on the sentiment of people that any change of whatever kind on the the Kingship will be but a change on Nepal and the Nepalese people.

Thus, the people of Nepal never took the monarchy for an impediment to the development of the country and its democracy; rather, they have marched ahead on the path of progress under the leadership of the Crown, seeing to the need of the time. It is this fundamental element on the merit of which the Nepalese people revere the King and the King has won maximum popularity. The King of Nepal, as the monarch of Britain, cannot be impeached. The kingship in Nepal, therefore, is an office of supreme honour. The honour of our nationality consists but in the honour of the Crown, which is the only basis of our nationality.

H.J. Laski, the famous socialist politician of England has sharply criticised Monarchy in the following words:—"The whole trend of social and economic evolution since the war has brought into discussion the foundation of social organisation. To take a wide view of the royal authority is to invoke it as a weapon capable at least of postponing and perhaps of preventing any change in the nature of those foundations. There is no doubt that the prerogative of the king seems to men both of eminence and experience in politics above all a means of delaying the coming of socialism. "Now the same Laski says, "The roots of monarchy lies deep in human experience. To bring its foundations into dispute is to raise controversies of which no one foresee the end.

It is such a truth as has proved very important in the politics of almost all monarchical states of the world. Great historic changes took place in the politics of all those states, where question of monarchy was raised as a subject of controversy.

Professor Laski viewed the special right of the King as an element impeding the coming in of socialism and that he did in the state where monarchy has proved helpful in the development of democracy and stood as a symbol of democracy in the process of development. But in Nepal the Crown, the founder of democracy, has been offering leadership to the people for advancement on the path of progress rather than it has come to be worth being called socialistic. The encouraging works done under the leadership of the King so as to improve the lot of the working class by doing away with the economic inequality through the media of the agricultural (reform the principal pillar of the present Nepalese economic position) and the introduction of the cooperative system, and in order to dispel the social evils and inequality by the enforcement of the "MulkiAin" (civil code) are not at all less progressive than any socialistic reform. These works are "reforms" and they are revolutionary rather than socialistic. So to attempt at comparing the Crown of Nepal with the Crown in any country of the world is to show the want of the knowledge of its real importance. The afore—said socialistic refroms brought to effect in Nepal make it obvious that even the King can be the leader of socialism.

In Nepal, it is the Crown that threads all the Nepalese politics on one and same string stands as a symbol of national unity, stability, prosperity and honourable fame; this is quite beyond controversy. It has won the faith and loyality of the entire Nepalese population. The good of the people as enunciated by the demand of time and the sentiment of the people is the good of the King, and in his Voice and feelings alone are the voices of the people echoed and their feeling reflected. Right till today this very philosophy has remained the radical formula of the successful monarchical tradition in Britain.

Unification alone is the most elemental agency that saves a nation from falling into catastrophe, and, in Nepal, not only the material unification, but also the unification of the power of the people and the political and spiritual unifications of the country have issued from the Crown.

Ever after Paush 1, 2017, Nepal has made an unprecedented amount of progress in the growth of national spirit. Even the several temporary governments that came to exist after 2007 had, no doubt, striven after the unification and development of this national spirit, but they failed to achieve success in their attempts. The reason for the failure is obvious. They lacked in influentiality and capability. Their influence were strictly confined to party politics.

After 2017, the unification and development of the entire national spirit could easily take place on the call for them by the Crown. It is an outcome of the greatness and influentiality of the Crown and of the sacred faith of the people in the Crown as well. It is, at the same time a brilliant example of the truth that national well-being and security lies safe and unimpaired in the leadership of the Crown.

That the monarchical system of government is, where it exists as a tradition, the most influential and the republican system the weakest is best known on the practical experiences gained of both the systems. Monarchy has proved very capable of bringing about unity in the country. In India, the centre has been made constitutionally very powerful. It has been made so with an end to do away with the national weakness of the republican system. In times of national emergency the entire power of the republic constitutionally concentrates itself on the centre; and, under such a circumstance, India comes to be more like a unitary state. When any national crisis is to be coped with all national powers come to be centralised under one unchallangable authority. In Nepal, however, the Crown has always remained the symbol and reflection of nationality.

In the universal history of national awakening and reconstruction Nepal has played a pioneer role. This can so be affirmed, because Nepal is the only country which could feel national reawakening in all its nerves and has been undertaking the colossal task of national rebuilding under the leadership of the Crown. In the history of the world, the 17th century marks concurrence of the decay of the Medieval knowledge and the genesis of the modern political philosophy. The decay and the genesis were essentially two historically important consequences of the Renaissance, as other consequences whereof social, political and economic developments took place, and a religious movements issued in Europe. As a substantial outcome of these consequences, development of national spirits in various countries in the continent made itself easy.

Inspite of the fact that the feudal system continued to exist in Europe till the French Revolution in 1789 and in Russia till the revolution of 1917, it may be asserted that it had started to break up gradually much earlier in most countries as a result of the intellectual revival and the reformation. In the 18th century evalution of states indoctrinated in nationalism took place. To meet the demand of the age Nepal obtained the leadership of the Crown. Under the leadership of King Prithvi Narayana Shah, Nepal, a minor state in Asia, led the entire continent to a new awakening. "The national revolution of Nepal took place 33 years prior to the American war of independence and 46 years earlier than French Revolution."

It was, thus under the leadership of the Crown that Nepal proved a pioneer in the sphere of leadership for the new awakening. It was through the efforts of king Prithvi Narayana Shah that it stood up as a well-knit shate. It may, therefore, be said that it is the Crown that has assumed the foremost revolutionary leadership historically momentous, for boosting Nepal and the Nepalese to completely new environments becoming of the ages.

In most countries of the world either long conflicts have issued between the Crown and the people or blood had been shed for the rights of the latter. But history of Nepal has remained deadly opposed to both the conflicts and bloodshed. In Nepal, the people have gone even to the extent of endangering their lives for the safeguard of the rights of the King and the King too, on his part, has exposed his throne and dear life for the sake of the restoration of the rights of the people. The political knowledge that any statesman endeavours to comprehend the Nepalese politics without at all taking note of this speciality of the Nepalese Crown will lent be incomplete.

The Nepalese monarchy has met the demand of the age by taking the fearless lead in giving the country up-to-date laws and reforms concerning land, which makes it clear that the monarchy in Nepal is not a feudal institution. Having a through understanding of the demand of the age, the King has, by taking proper, advanced measures, shown the Nepalese monarchy as a progressive institution. In Nepal, the courage, effortfulness and worthy leadership of the monarch have combined to set athwart feudalism and traditionalism and thereby paved a wide way for progress through new reforms becoming of the age, and consequently a first-grade social atmosphere is in the making. On the background of this very change the genuine kind and mode of the Nepalese monarchy have come to reveal themselves fully According to Dr. Tulsi Giri, former Chairman of the Council of Ministers, absolute monarchy is illustrative of feudalism, and constitutional monarchy symbolic of inertness and weakness; but since, in Nepal, the monarchy should offer and is offering an active, up-to-date leadership, there are in the leadership of the present monarch an original, genuine mark and a special quality quite away from any one of the aspects pointed out above.

The Nepalese history of the past 12 years has pointed out this that mere theoretical know-how and divine rights of kings will not help the society or the country to obtain the leadership of the desired kind, nor will any king affixing primary importance to public role and secondary moment to himself, be in a position to fulfil the needs of the Nepalese. The part that the King is playing active leadership of the nation, too, has only proved. Dr. Giri's explanation true. The unshakable determination shown by the role played by the King on a detachment from feudalism to an adaptation to completely new social, economic and political environments has much enhanced the faith of the Nepalese people in the monarch. This is, in fact, a healthy analysis of the monarchy in Nepal.

But that even constitutional monarchy may be active has been elucidated by the truth pertaining to the Nepalese monarchy. Therefore, only that alone which is, till, today customarily called constitutional monarch, may be said to be inactive. The Nepalese monarchy, inspite of its being constitutional, is very active.

Sovereignty: At this point, however, this question may arise: If the Nepalese monarchy is constitutional, wherein lies the sovereignty of the state? But the answer to the question is ripe and ready—the sovereignty of Nepal is constitutionally vested in the King. All executive, legislative and judicial rights issue from him.

The state is an organisation. A collective body of individuals constitutes a union or association or organisation; but when its individual members are taken as separate identities, no organization will fall to individual fractions. If we break an organization composed of a hundred members into a hundred separate individuals, none of the hundred individuals will bear hundredth part of the organisation. An organisation is formed when individuals combine; it ceases to exist as soon as the combination of individuals is disbanded. Even then the all-in-all leader of the organisation is or can be a king of supreme individual or group of individuals. But, when compared to a state or nation it is but an abstract, temporary, unauthentic and incomplete example. The state is permanent and well-founded on political, spiritual, social and geographical factors. This organization in the form of the state possesses a collective power, which, in the political terminology, is called 'sovereignty. This power in Nepal is vested in the King. In Nepal, the Crown is sovereign and permanent. It is a symbol of national organisation and the supreme leader of the kingdom. The sovereignty of Nepal vested in the King, with the King not as an individual but as the head of the Kingdom of Nepal, the big political family of all the Nepalese. The source of the sovereignty vested in the King rests, in fact, with the common people.

A study of the words "...in exercise of the sovereign powers and prerogatives inherent in us according to the constitutional law, custom and usage of our country and which devolved on us from our August and Revered Forfathers......", occurring in the last paragraph of the Preamble of the constitution of 2019, it may lead a critic to comment that, since the words put it clear that the Nepalese sovereignty does not emanate from the people but takes its rise from the constitutional law, custom and usage of the country, such an old trend in the concept of sovereignty cannot be harmonized with the democratic principles of today but stands out as a symbol of the Medieval theory of the divine rights of kings. But a careful study of the words will reveal the reality. In the age when the divine rights of kings were so much revered popular will was nothing valuable; and no question was at all raised as to its importance. But today the exercise of the sovereign powers and prerogatives by His Majesty, because the exercise is in full agreement with the spirit of the words, "...powers are exercised by His Majesty through the organs established by or under this constitution and other laws for the time being in force keeping in view the interest and wishes of the subjects," occurring in article 20(2) of the constitution of 2019, is both constitutional and democratic. Since the

Preamble of the constitution of 2019 also says, "...it is desirable in the best interest and for all round progress......of the Nepalese people to conduct the government of the country in consonance with the popular will...and in keeping with the national genius and traditions, and as originating from the very base with the active co-operation of the whole people..." it is obvious that the vestment of the sovereign powers in the King is not contrary to the popular will. The popular will is the backbone of modern democracy. If the popular will is constitutionally recognised as basis of government, then it can never be allaged that the vestment is not fully democratic.

To any democratic principle the question "how are the sovereign powers exercised?" is more mementous than the question "To whom should they be entrusted?". In Britain, the powers vested in the monarch are less significant constitutionally than the way in which they are exercised. In India, the sovereign powers of the President are less important themselves than how they are wielded. In Nepal the sovereign powers rest with His Majesty, but their exercise is strictly in keeping with the popular will and therefore constitutional and democratic. The objective behind the powers and prerogatives of the King, because it is to accomplish "happiness and prosperity of the people, is, beyond doubt, fully democratic. Even on ground of the words "......powers and prerogatives inherent in us according to the constitutional law, custom and usage..." in the preamble of the constitution of 2019 we cannot accept the three elements, *viz.* the constitutional law, custom and usage, as the sources of the Nepalese sovereignty. These elements only recognize the powers inherent in His Majesty; in other words, a careful study of them will through light on the truth that the vestment of the sovereign powers in the King have got the recognition of "the constitutional law, custom and usage" of the country.

The form of the Nepalese monarchy is, in reality, so typical, and characteristic that it does not account the King as a separate identity; rather it insists on keeping the county, the King and the people as a single whole, an entire trinitry. This single whole has got the people in its organisational aspect, the country in its geographical aspect, and the King in its sovereign aspect; and it is the king that symbolises the material leadership of the nation. So the sovereignty of the country pervades the entire population, and its expression is manifest in the King. It is on this ground that it could be asserted that the sovereignty of Nepal is vested in the King. As a matter of fact, no comment of any kind whatever can be entertained with recourse to the say that there lies with the King a separate sovereignty, not at all related to the people. Even during the Rana regime, the sovereignty of the country rested with the King. At this point, however, there arises a question as to the relationship between rights and duties of the King. In any modern democratic system rights and duties are taken as two important foctors that go together Rights void of duties are not considered justified. Rights of all kinds conferred on the King by the constitution, but the constitution makes no mention of the duties of the King. Comments, placing the King and the entire Nepalese population quite apart from each other, have, therefore, come to hearing. But the constitution considers duties more important for the safeguard of the rights. The words of the King, the founder of Panchayat philosophy, that *in the Panchayat system as much importance is attached to duties as is attached to rights are worth special mention here*. There are critics who assent that the Constitution also must make definite mentions of the duties of the supreme ruler of the state. But it will be better, if they once again critically examine the constitutional positions of the king and the president of the democratic states of Great Britain and India before they pass any more comment or criticism on the subject.

Since popular will is the backbone of democracy, no system of government can be said to be democratic unless it has won its support. It is for this reason that popular will commands so prominent position in the constitution of Nepal, and that it has been deemed desirable to conduct the government according to its dictates. This, however, signals at the duties of the one holding the sovereign powers and points it out as his duty to rule the country on the authority of the popular will. Since in the Preamble of the constitution mentions of the popular will precedes that of the sovereign powers, the precedence gives the covert suggestion of "duties before rights". All democratic rights fall in toto under and consist in popular will. It must be mentioned here that the sovereign powers vested in the King are regulated by "Rajdharma". It is a peculiar characteristic quality of the Nepalese monarchy.

His Majesty, King Mahendra, toured the different nooks of the country, and, through his close personal contacts with the people he acquired a first-hand knowledge of their problems and hardships and difficulties. This won him the hearts of his people and put him forward as a historical national leader and as a king beloved of his subjects. The history of the world with hardly have an instance paralled to this.

His tours of the various parts of the world has made clear to all that King Mahendra has always been effortful for pushing his country honourably ahead into the world of internationalism and establishing and promoting Nepal's friendly relations with various other countries of the world. Through his tour of the world Nepal has come to occupy an important state in the stage of the international politics. Good-will visits to other countries of the world is very instrumental for a country to promote its friendly relations with them. King Edward VII of England paid his visits to many states, and it was for reason of these good-will visits that the war with Germany could be sworn off. This toil of Edward VII had proved subservient to the popularization of the British monarchy. Now, since the credit for the renown and reputation of Nepal in the international sphere of life should go to King Mahendra, it must beowned by the Nepalese populace that his good-will visits to many countries of the world has enhanced the popularity and prestige of the Nepalese Crown.

The Revolution of 2017 resulted more significantly than the Revolution of 2007. If the revolution of 2007 was like a conjunction of the decay of the ancient feudalism and the dawn of a new democratic beginning, the Revolution of 2017 was a democratic national revolution, full of events and historically very important. Both the revolutions were led by the Crown, both had the brave Nepalese people as fighters, and the objective behind both was to create a democratic environment for Nepal and the Nepalese people. Both were successful; for both had fairly obtained the co-operation of the Crown and the people.

After 2007 the political parties began to scramble for power. They saw to it that their motifs alone were served. They roused unnecessary political clamours and brought the country on to the verge of anarchy. All these handicapped the proper utilization of democratic principles. This state of affairs rendered it inevitable for the King to stop the devaluation of the sacred spirit of toil and sacrifice displayed in the revolution 2007 and to check the Nepalese people who had just moved a step forward in the path of democracy from receding per force to the darkness of undemocratic ignorancy. Any revolution in any other country could hardly get so complete and so unanimous support of the entire population as King Mahendra got from his people in 2017. The historic Royal lead in the Revolution was the reflex of the voices of the people.

Through the Revolution of 2007 put an end to the ancient feudal system, yet certain sources of feudalism did continue to operate. These sources had got to be dried up. Even after the Revolution of 2017, the King took revolutionizing reformatory measures in the forms of the Land Reform Act and the new Mulki Laws to turn down the still active sources of feudalism, which came to style the Nepalese Crown as progressive and democratic. If these reformatory steps of his may be looked upon as symbolic of socialism, the King of Nepal can very well be regarded as the leader of socialism. It is for this reason that the Crown has come to win the hearts of the Nepalese people as a popular rebellion. To dry up the deep-laid sources of feudalism was a more difficult task than to bring feudalism itself to a close. It required fundamental economic and social reconstruction, which has started since the Revolution of 2017 on the merits of the co-operation between the King and the people.

Narendra Goel, an Indian writer, commenting upon the various aspects of the Constitution of 2015, interprets the Nepalese monarchy as one of the two parties to the political drama of Nepal. He takes as "Parties to this drama, the monarch and the people's representatives". But this assumption of his is contrary to the Nepalese reality. Since, in Nepal, the, Crown is the root power in possession of the entire sovereignty to fancy it to be a party is totally wrong. To make the monarch a party antagonistic to the party of the people's representatives in the politics of Nepal and thereby to leave the Crown a subject of debate and controversy cannot be said to be true to the Nepalese tradition and reality. He further writes in his comments that the history of the time since the Revolution of 2007 showed no political party having proved itself more progressive than the King and that the "political leaders of the country showed little talent of leadership or statemanship during the past years of their free rule and government after the revolution of 2007. He has drawn a number of conclusions from an account of the brief political and contitutional history which he has traced previous to commenting on the various aspects of the constitution. And some of the conclusions he has drawn are as follow:

1. The King of Nepal was anti-Ranarchy popular leader of the Revolution and won for the Crown the revered honour, "Father of the Nation".
2. The King universally honoured by the entire population of the Kingdom of Nepal.
3. The leader of the country showed little leadership and statesmanship.
4. In the changing and instable political condition of the country, "the King acquired a role of guiding democracy".
5. Thus, the monarchy obtained "double justification" for its existence and increasing powers and rights.

The history of many countries have shown that an instable government allowed to continue for a long time paves the way for military dictatorship in the long run. Even though the Nepali Congress won the election, nobody could disclaim internal dissensions in it or guarantee their absence from it. Under such a circumstance, the wielding of his discretionary powers by a King does not seem improper only if the wielding aims at meeting an emergency.

Thus, Mr. Goel seems to have arrived at approximately axact conclusions, but his conclusions are drawn upon his private precepts.

As a matter of fact, the King of Nepal is the protector of the welfare of the country, of the well-being of the people, and of the constitution. It was imperative for the history of Nepal since 2017 to keep the ultimate discretionary powers secure in the King, so that it might teach the political parties the lession that the idological differences and scrambles for prower between them and their private interests and lack of foresight might lead the country down to adversity. This power of the King to use his discretion is very much similar to the constitutional rights guaranteed to the heads of the democratic countries like the United States, Great Britain and India. This history of the past few years has made it manifest that it has never impeded the free working of the leaders of the people, that it was exercised ultimately only for saving the country from political disaster, and that the ultimate exercise was done as a response to the demand of the people in general. The powers and prerogatives vested constitutionally in the King have been exercised in normal conditions only in consultation with the Ministers in the Cabinet. It has been mentioned above that His Majesty has never returned, by exercising his discretionary powers, any bill presented to him for his assent either by the parliament (when it was existent) or by the National Panchayat. All other works have been done by the ministers themselves in the name of the King. This has been the tradition of any monarchical democratic system.

Analyzing the role of the Nepalese monarchy, Mr. Goel has stated that its fruenctions seem to be to guide and lead the new-born democracy, to make it up-to-date and progressive, and to accomplish national unity and stability. This analysis based on the history of Nepal since 2007, cannot be said to have been in the wrong.

Dissensions and scrambles took place within the ruling party itself and among the parties. The political parties attached greater moment to their interests than to the well-being of the country and the people. The coming of as many as six governments within a brief period of five years created an instable political atmosphere. Under these circumstances the efforts of the Crown alone gave life to the new-born democracy from the political chaos. The leaders of the political parties, who fought as brave soldiers in the Revolution, kept engaged in scrambles and tugs-of war amongst themselves. The national leader of the Revolution, the King, was, as an impartial umpire seeing to it that the very rights of the leaders and their parties not prove fatal to the new-born democracy. When the people placed a demand for a general election, the king got the election held; and abiding by the democratic tradition, entrusted the chance of organizing the government to the winning party and placed upon its shoulders the responsibility of governing the country. Analyzing the real position of the political leaders then, Mr. Gole writes, "There was a furtive attempt to raise an agitation to force the issue of general elections, but when the date of election was announced by the King some of the ministers and erstwhile leaders pleaded for postponment on various ground:

Even to-day, in many civilized and progressive countries of the world; *e.g.* Britain, Japan, Denmark and Iran, the monarchical system holds good. Had the monarchy in any of them been opposed to the welfare of the people and the development of the country, the people there need not at all glory in the monarchy they have. It will not be prudent and logical to-day to speak in favour of the continuity of the monarchy in a country, when it has been quite evident that not even a big empire in this age of democracy can remain firm and stable, if it goes and operates against the wish and will of its people. It is not democratic in spirit to-day for any people to any that other countries should be prevailed upon to have the same kind of the political institution which their country has and to call it alone democratic. This comes to be just a pampered sentiment with the breath of imperialism or colonialism.

A symbol to any extent, large or small, the king is, after all, a man; and the relation of the King to his ministers is the relation of man to man. If a King likes do a work, will it not have its impact on his ministers? If a King, however little symbolic, loves to perform some task for the welfare of his country, will it be practically possible for his ministers to overlook it? These two questions are of great importance to a student of political science. "Even the most symbolic King is not wooden, if he has a will of his own, and constitutional in any case is a matter of human relationship between the King and his cabinet." Therefore, monarchy has still been continuing in many countries because of its approval by the people and by virtue of its being not detrimental but instrumental to the development of the country and the people. In Nepal, the will and pleasure of the King has been for the well-being of the country and the people and for the development of perfect democracy and welfare state as well. So here the will of the King is in reality, a reflex of the popular will. This is again what the constitutional guarantee of the discretionary powers to the King actually means. Even in a democratic state like Britain, the monarch is the focus of patriotism and a source of inspiration for the common people. In Nepal too, the Crown has been alive focus of patriotism during times of political instability. The following royal good will has been synonymous to the welfare of the country and the well—being of the people:

> "It has been my profound wish that the Nepalese people be smiling, and be nice in their deals with others......My sole desire is to find all my beloved subjects, rich or poor, happy by all means. My only prayer to Lord Almighty is that His unbounded grace may ever make me able to live or die for the sake of the country and the people." Whatever others

may think of the King who enkindled the spirits of patriotism and nationality among his people by saying, "*The country is a common property of all. Without the country, we are nothing...If the existence of Nepal is wiped off, we, as the Nepalese, are wiped off too......I too have some duties to perform, which consists in protecting all works done for the good of the country and the well-being of the people*" and who with an open heart called for the co-operation of the people by making the utterance:

> "*If any real impediment comes to stand in the way of protecting any work done for the good of the country, I shall never deter from doing whatever will be deemed necessary for surmounting the impediment, for which I seek the co-operation of the Nepalese alone.*"

The Nepalese people do obey him as their protector, leader, guide and one beloved of them. And all Nepalese people have already marched forward under the leadership of the monarch who testified to his resoluteness by saying.

> "*Once I have come afield on my firm determination to 'make' our beautiful country, Nepal, by performing the sacred duty of working for all the people of the country, I must not shrink back from performing that duty.*"

This ideal leadership for the development of democracy has made the Crown very popular among the people. From this we arrive at the conclusions that in Nepal the Crown has turned the popular background very important and that the importance of the very popular background has heightened the moment of the Crown.

Y.G. Krishnamurti, an author of repute, says, "politics of King Mahendra has broken the barrier between the ruler and his people." From the leadership of King Mahendra has emanated a new political consciousness which before 2017, could not flow out of any political party or organization. According to what Mr. Krishnamurti has opined, political parties 'are' essential for modern democracy, but the parties in Nepal could not prepare the necessary atmosphere. "The political analyst could see that unscrupulous leadership hatched a plot to push off the King and convert Nepal into the junior partner of a neighbouring-power political state." Thus only after nationality and existence had come to challange each other, King Mahendra took the venture some historic step and made has already popular leadership more popular.

'King' and 'the revolutionary' are two antagonistic terms. But in the personality of the King of Nepal we discover a duality; in other words, the ruler of Nepal is both the King and the revolutionary. Mr. Krishnamurti calls it "a scene unequalled in the modern world". That is why no Crown of any other State can come to stand in comparison with the Crown of Nepal. The history of Nepal since 2017 has put it doubtless to the Nepalese people that, if the King had not led the situation into his command during the days of emergency, even the existence of Nepal would be endangered. It is for this reason that King Mahendra may be said to be one of those unique historic kings who have won the boundless faith and esteem of their people. It is through his historic achievements that the leadership of the Nepalese Crown has come to be developed and cultured in a way becoming of the present age. All statesmen have been acquainted with the truth that Nepal and the Nepalese do what their monarch does.

Party politics breaks up the intellectual power of the country and fractionizes the potentialities of the people. Especially in underdeveloped countries, party politics has been found obstructive to the desired rates of speed in the sketching or implementations of all-round development and construction programmes based on the unity and national spirit of the country. So on Pauch 22,2017, King Mahendra, by a royal declaration, laid ban on all political parties and all class organizations motivated from party politics. Three years after this in Chitra, 2020, (corresponding to April, 1964)—the Ne Win government of Burma Socialist Programme Party banned all other parties by enforcing the National Solidarity Act, March, 1964. The enforcement of the National Solidarity Act in Burma is an important incident in the history of Asia after 1960. This incident is a warning to other countries of Asia that are underdeveloped, where political leaders profess party democracy alone as the main formula for progress. The partiless political philosophy founded by King Mahendra was entirely for Nepal. But in the context of the measure taken by the Ne Win government in Burma, it has placed itself important in the politics of the Sonth-East Asia.

King Mahendra, the propounder of Panchayat philosophy, was cent per cent in a favour of the parliamentary system. This is evident by the constitutional provisions he made for the general election of 2015. But finding that the egoism and self-centred attitudes of the parties polutted the political atmosphere of the country, he had to take the historic measure of Pausha 1,2017. Throwing light on the necessity of leading the country to a charged light of a new political philosophy unhindered by the self-portraying tendencies of the political parties looking forward only to their own interests, he had said, "For the purpose that the people may not be subjected to suffering under the powers of any political party, a Panchayat system, befitting the soil and tradition of our country has been arranged. "The good wish of the King to make Nepal a welfare state did not seem possible in a party—democracy, and so the new system of the Panchayat came to be adopted. Since it rests in the ultimate responsibility of the Crown not only to protect democracy at all costs but also" to save the national unity and sovereignty of the country, to maintain and preserve peace in the country, and to stop the country from any possible deterioration." King Mahendra, having an eye to the well-being of the country and the welfare of the people, gave his subject the Panchayat democratic philosophy thereby leading them on to real democracy, and much enhanced the popularity of the Crown. In England to-day the monarch is regarded as a demi-god for his works for the well-being of the state and welfare of his subjects. "Some of tributes devoted to the person of the monarch since the war would certainly have been more suited to the description of a demi-god than to the actual occupants of the throne in the last sixty years." In England, the keen patriot sentiments of the monarchs like Queen Victoria and Edward VII and their works for the good of the state, and the victory offered publicly to George V have largely contributed to enhancing the prestige of the Crown; and this is a remarkable achievement of the popularity of British monarchy.

It cannot however, be said that the monarchies in other states should be modelled on the British pattern. The monarchy in any other state may, in spite of its constitutional affinity to its British counterpart, be entirely different by its position and tradition from it in many respects. In England, no party at all made any 'appeal to the royal authority in any final way' to solve even the grave problems in a way at once favourable to it. We may cite as examples of the problems two very important issues in British history—the burning questions concerning the creation of the Pears in the House of Lords (1910—11) and the Ulster Crisis (1913-14). But in Nepal, the political parties approached the royal authority for the solutions of even minor problems in ways benefitial to them. So the King of Nepal had to be active as an impartial umpire between contending interests. Had the King been inactive in the name of constitutional monarchy, the struggles among the political parties for the accomplishments of their respective desires for their own private weal would result very ill, and nobody could say what sort of future there would be in, for Nepal. From this it is clear that the very political circumstances in Nepal have made the monarchy very active.

In Nepal, the Crown is the symbol of nationality and national unity. Here the Crown is integrated air—tight to the country and the people. The Crown, the country and the people together constitute a single whole—a trinity. Each specific one-third of the single whole is a definite aspect of it, the people forming the organizational aspect, the country, the geographic aspect; and the Crown the sovereign aspect. To question the authority of the Crown, therefore, is "to debate the existence of

Nepal, the Nepalese and Nepalese nation. "The great royal utterance that if the existence of Nepal is wiped off, the Nepalese will be wiped off too, is the expression of this very truth. Therefore no person, loving Nepal and the Nepalese can bring the Crown to a subject of debate and discussion.

Only one person represents the Crown or monarchy. The representative is called the king. The king, because he represents the Crown, commands unbounded esteem of the people. In Nepal, the sovereign powers are constitutionally vested in the King. All the powers emanate from him. It cannot, be argued that the King, the object of worship, devotion and esteem of the Nepalese people can be a subject of debate. No Nepali likes to make the beloved King, who loves and affects his people, a subject of argument. Even according to the modern traditions of constitutional monarch, the Crown of the King cannot be a topic of controversy. The following revolutioning sentences of His Majesty, King Mahendra, are introductory to his progressiveness, liberality and greatness:

> "Now that my sole aim in life has been to accomplish happiness and prosperity of the people and the country. I wish that all, urged by their patriotic impulses but devoid of personal interests, make solid criticisms and hold healthy discussions with open hearts."
>
> "I do not feel abashed to confess to my flaws, if they are flaws at bottom; for if I have any interest of my own, that I have for the good of the country and the people."

A student of political science may say that in England they talk openly on or about the monarch. Right in the parliament too they may held discussions as to the Crown. "It is not without significance," says Prof. Laski, "that the official daily newspaper of the Trade Union Congress devotes more space, of the news and pictures, to the royal family than does any of its rivals." What Prof. Laski says is not a thing less important.

But it is difficult to say on the merits of what has just been mentioned above that the king can become a topic of debate.

Talks on or about the king alone cannot make him a subject of controversy. The famous English saw, that the King can do no wrong, is a proof of the fact that in England the monarch cannot be a subject of debate.

This is just an example. As a matter of fact the Nepalese tradition, the matchless history of the monarchy and the deep sense of esteem and reverence that the Nepalese people have for their monarch, have together put the Nepalese King above all comparisons with the other kings of the world.

From these facts, therefore, we can arrive at the following conclusions:

1. The Crown of Nepal is an age—old glorious tradition: and as such it has blended itself inseparably with the hereditary psychology of the Nepalese people. Also in other monarchical states, kings have their lasting impacts upon societies.
2. As an impartial umpire: the Crown of Nepal has seen to it that the political games are played according to the code of rules. When the King found that the games were played foul, he, unlike any other constitutional monarch, gave an active guidance to the players, so that they might play fair to the utmost satisfaction of his own and of the expectant spectators.
3. The King never got himself tangled into party politics; and, the well-being of the people and the unity of the nation being his objectives, has, in times of national emergency, saved the country from political devastation.
4. Even the cabinet system of government has never and in no state been found conducted without one person as the supreme head of the state. Therefore, even though monarchy is dissolved in a state, some person preferably other than the one who held the sceptre, most he stayed as the head of the state. The person thus elected for holding the supreme powers of the state does not continuously hold the reins. After a brief period of time

another person must be elected to the replacement of the one in office.

The election may require lots of expenses: and, moreover, the head of the state, say the President, thus elected may be bereft of such attractive smartness, personality and greatness to maintain and preserve national unity, stability and glory, as a king can in a country having a glorious tradition can possess. When some one must be recognised and empowered as the supreme head of the state, why should a country not continue to have the monarchy which is glorious, traditionally iilustrated and historically befitted into the socio-political sentiments of the people? This question embodies the reversed recognition accorded to constitutional monarchy. This is the fundamental principle of the cabinet system of government that the "formal head of the state" should not participate in party politics, nor should he enter into any political controversy. A constitutional monarch is farther off from party politics than on elected President. In the words of Prof. Jyoti Prasad Sood, people may believe that he works being fully independent of party control. According to the British writer of repute Mr. Jennings, a constitutional monarch is profitably independent of the party control. A statesman who is elected as President, cannot forget his past. If he at all forgets it, others in the party of which he is a member cannot forget it. But this does not mean that a hereditary king is flawless. As Prof. Sood observes in his book, "Great Britain Ki Shasan Vyavastha" (The Administrative system in Great Britain), disadvantages are there of hereditary Kingship but advantages are there too in a greater number. In his book, "The British Constitution": Mr. Jennings puts it in clear words that the President cannot be an alternative to the Crown. Since in Nepal the existence of the Crown and the combined existence of Nepal and the Nepalese nation are tightly independent, to fancy an alternative to the Crown is to fancy the end of Nepal and the Nepalese people.

5. Because Nepal is the only Hindu sovereign kingdom the King of Nepal is a symbol of the Aryan culture.
6. The Nepalese monarchy is a queer combination of antiquity and modernity. Right till now the King is looked upon as an incarnation of God. Unlike in other monarchical states of the world, the King in Nepal has given the Country a new democratic system and, according to the demand of the age the progressive social and economic reforms. This is a special characteristic of the Nepalese monarchy.
7. In Nepal, the sacrifice of the monarch, his affection for the people, his hard work and his foresight have all combined to transform the monarchy into a progressive institution. His courage and farsightedness have changed the very run of the history of Nepal, and has bravely turned the sequence of events to a country's well-being and the successful working of democracy.
8. In Nepal, the monarchy has been made revered and popular more by the powerful religious and historical traditions than by politics. The theory of the divine rights of kings is now obsolete. The very fight against the divine rights gradually gave rise to the principle that the governmental authority cannot transgress certain original rights of the people. This very principle later developed into the theory of the fundamental rightsto be guaranteed to the people. So to-day's theory of the fundamental rights is a gift of the modern age, which had taken its rise from the strife against the divine rights of kings. Till now the King is worshiped as God in Nepal. The king has never made even the least attempt at working against the feelings and sentiments of the people, nor has he ever tried, even to the least to be disrespectful to the rights of the people. There has risen no question, again, on the side of the people, of struggle with the king for their fundamental rights. On

the contrary, the people have ever obtained the co-operation of the king in all important matters concerning the respect of and leadership for their sentiments. That the Nepalese people obtained the leadership of the Crown for gaining their rights and in their safeguard is a landmark in the history of monarchy in the world. It is on account of this historical tradition that in Nepal monarchy has grown so popular and the Crown has become symbolic of the popular sentiment. It is for this reason that the interdependence of the existences of Nepal and the Nepalese has come to eastablish itself as a basic factor in the Nepalese politics. After the historic happening of 2017 all statesmen might have come to understand the factor as a truth. On this firm background of the popular sentiment and spirit the Nepalese monarchy founded.

9. The esteem for or faith in the King exceeds with force from the popular sentiment as its source, whereas the regard for the President comes off only as a duty dictated according to some definite political ideology. This is a truth based upon individual human psychology.

10. In Nepal, the Crown is a symbol of nationality, and sovereign integrity. The Nepalese history so far has put it transparent clear that, without the greatness, influence and attraction of the Crown, Nepal will disintegrate, communal and regional antagonisms will prevail and aggregate themselves, and the very existence of Nepal will be endangered.

11. The King has never and nowhere called the democratic trend of thought "Utopian." On every word and on every stop of his are reflected the true spirits of democracy; and from this democratic trends have drawn much inspiration. The King himself has taken the lead in effecting peacefully the revolutionizing changes. Democratic recognitions individual liberty, respect for the individual and justice—have got much

inspiration from the King; and these recognitions, they are the principle foundations of the Panchayat system. Nobody can disavow this truth.

12. Ever since the government of the country began to be conducted constitutionally, any measure taken by the King came to be duly confined to constitutional limits. The King never oversteped the resolutions of the house of people's representatives. In each work and measure of the King, the popular background played an important role. Such a good settled behaviour of the King has made it obvious that he has always respected the popular role, and democratic recognition and tradition the important elements in the political trends of the modern age.

13. "The Evening Standard" a celebrated British newspaper once wrote, "He (King Mahendra) might have been an absolute ruler, but instead he chooses to guide his peoples towards managing their own affairs."

The following royal utterances have been giving full inspiration to the vigilance of the Nepalese poeple:

"Our very wish for the decentralization of power is indicative of our continued faith in democracy." "Unless and until the people themselves are vigilant, conscious and active, their well-being cannot be materialized.

14. In fact, the moment we, to-day, hear or mention the term "monarchy" we necessarily call to mind the monarchy in Great Britain. But in respect of the two terms, "monarchy" and "King" there does not exist in any other respect any likeness between the monarchy in Great Britain and the monarchy in Nepal. The monarch in Great Britain is just a titular ruler or mere ornament of the constitution, while the Nepalese monarchy is an energetic leader, a vigilant guard over democracy, a revolutionary leader of the people, and the founder of a new lively political philosophy. The

British monarch may just be cited only as an iliustration, not as an institution bearing resemblance to its Nepalese counterpart. The Nepalese Crown. on the background of the Panchayat philosophy, surpasses in comparison any other Crown of the world.

2

King Mahendra and Political Development

From 1955 to 1959 King Mahendra had been an unusually active ruler, holding protracted negotiations with political leaders, exercising a close supervision over Cabinet and Secretariat, and undertaking extensive tours within Nepal and abroad. His direct participation in the processes of government imparted a new political dimension to the Crown, in contrast with the essentially constitutional role assumed by his predecessor. But the political system envisaged under the 1959 Constitution could function only if the crown relegated itself to a less central role. The results of the general elections reinforced this situation in certain respects. The absence of a strong opposition party, for instance, deprived the Crown of the leverage with which to counterbalance the ruling party within the constitutional system itself without recourse to more drastic steps such as the full use of the Crown's executive and emergency powers or, under extreme provocation, suspension of the Constitution. Thus the future of parliamentary democracy was contingent upon the degree of mutual trust and toleration that could be engendered between the Nepali Congress leadership and the Crown.

KING MAHENDRA AND THE NEPALI CONGRESS CABINET

King Mahendra experienced little apparent difficulty in making the transition to a constitutional role in 1959. His actions and public statements during this period would seem to have been motivated by a genuine desire to give the institution of parliamentary democracy an honest trial. Once it was clear that the Nepali Congress had won an absolute majority in the general elections, the King unhesitatingly initiated negotiations with B.P. Koirala on the organization of a government. At the same time he admonished several of the opposition leaders who had petitioned him to invalidate the elections, suggesting that they make use of available legal channels for the redress of their grievances.

B. P. Koirala seems to have been given a completely free hand in selecting his Cabinet and in creating the post of Deputy Prime Minister, for which there was no provision in the Constitution. This was a complete break with the role played by the Crown since 1955, when the usual pattern had been for the King to select the party candidates for the Cabinet after protracted negotiations and then combine those selected with a few royal nominees. None of these procedures was followed in 1959. There were no royal nominees, and the list of Cabinet members was drawn up by B. P. Koirala in consultation with the party. Indeed, the list was made public on May 20, one week before King Mahendra announced it officially. Further, the King dissolved the three high-powered administrative bodies he had formed in 1957 to assist him in the supervision of the government. This was widely interpreted as an indication of the King's intention to give a clean slate to the new Cabinet and to allow it to function without direct guidance from the royal palace. King Mahendra also cooperated with the new Cabinet by issuing two executive orders that enabled the government to function until all provisions of the 1959 Constitution had become operative. One of these orders permitted the administration to expend funds on its own authority until a budget had been approved by the Parliament; the other provided for the formation of a Cabinet before the selection of the Upper House of Parliament.

There was only one incident in this initial period in which the King's actions were potentially embarrassing to the Nepali Congress government. In announcing his list of nominees to the Senate on July 13, the King excluded all Nepali Congressmen except for three dissident party leaders. This was interpreted in some quarters as indicative of the King's desire to create an institutional counterbalance to the otherwise overwhelming predominance of the Cabinet within the Parliamentary system. But it can also be interpreted as a token of the King's concern for the broadest representation within the Parliament, only imperfectly achieved in the elections to the Lower House. All major ethnic and minority groups, including a Muslim and a woman, received representation on the Senate's nominated list.

The Palace Secretariat and the New Government

The assumption of broad administrative functions by the Crown in 1955 had led to what was in essence a dyarchical system of administration with two centers of decision making—one at the royal palace and the other at the Central Secretariat (Singha Darbar). The palace secretariat consisted of a complex hierarchy of civil and military officials, some inherited from King Tribhuwan's private staff and some newly recruited, and represented generally a diverse variety of interest groups. There were several important clusters within the palace staff, mostly centered around such factors as kinship relationships and ancestral service at the palace. But all these factions had a common interest in protecting their privileged and crucial decision-making position against the encroachment of the government functioning at the Central Secretariat.

Upon the installation of the Nepali Congress government in 1959, it was clear that the dyarchical pattern of administration was no longer viable. The palace secretariat had to be trimmed of its later accretions of administrative powers if it was to function primarily as a relay station between the King and the Cabinet, as originally intended by King Tribhuwan when he established a private secretariat in 1951. King Mahendra evidently sensed the potential conflict of interests and functions between the two secretariats under the new political system, for he moved to avert such a situation. He ordered the palace secretariat staff to pay their respects to Prime Minister Koirala at his residence shortly after the appointment of the new Cabinet. This formality was symptomatic of the new focus of political authority, and of the King's political perceptiveness.

This trend was reinforced by the care with which the Prime Minister established his personal authority over his colleagues in the Cabinet and thus, in effect, over the Central Secretariat. B. P. Koirala reserved for himself the right to report to the King on governmental affairs, and other members of the Cabinet could seek an audience with the King only with the permission of the Prime Minister. This was a clear break with past practices under which Ministers, and sometimes even Departmental Secretaries, had often sought private audiences with the King and had used these occasions to ventilate grievances against the Prime Minister or other colleagues with the inevitable consequence of endemic disharmony in the government. Presumably, the Prime Minister's ruling was resented in the palace secretariat, since it further restricted its scope of action, but King Mahendra seems to have accepted it as in conformity with his new constitutional status.

In October, 1959, an unprecedented episode took place in Kathmandu when King Mahendra participated in a football game at the invitation of Prime Minister Koirala. The sports event was held at the National Stadium and was open to the public. The proceeds from the game were donated to the Prime Minister's relief fund. King Mahendra and his brothers played on one side and the Prime Minister and his colleagues on the other. The political implications of the game were quickly noted by those sections of the press that were less than satisfied with the constitutional role of the King. To them King Mahendra's participation in the gaine was the result of a clever psychological assault, contrived by the Prime Minister, on the traditional prestige of the Crown. Other papers, which upheld the constitutional role of the King, hailed the event as one of historical importance not only "for the evolution of constitutional monarchy in Nepal, but also for the whole of the world." The debate raged with such intensity that King Mahendra felt it necessary to justify his participation. In a statement issued on the occasion he claimed that he had as much right as any other citizen to take part in public welfare activities, and added that inasmuch as games developed a spirit of unity they had an important role in promoting national progress.

In many respects King Mahendra's participation in a public sports event was the most dramatic confirmation of his role as a constitutional monarch. By temperament and habit he was easily the most serious-minded monarch Nepal had known for a long time. It was considered somewhat unusual, if not astounding, for him to condescend to play against his Ministers, who held their offices at his pleasure, in a football game. By tradition the King of Nepal is revered as the reincarnation of Vishnu—the Hindu god of preservation. King Mahendra had never publicly debunked this tradition; and for countless numbers of his subjects, the restoration of royal prerogatives in 1951 had meant a revivified faith in the divinity of the King. Mahendra's numerous trips throughout the country since his accession to the throne had brought this concept nearer to reality for his subjects, especially those who received quick dispensations of justice or royal favours of one kind or another. That King Mahendra took part in a football game and, more significantly, justified his role, was hailed by many observers as a prelude to a redefinition of the Crown's role in Nepali politics. It is possible that the Prime Minister and his colleagues subscribed to this view and drew up their future plans on the assumption that the constitutional role of the Crown was an accomplished and irrevocable fact.

The King and the Opposition

Opposition political parties organized a number of anti-government demonstrations in the fall and winter of 1959, but on what were obviously trivial or artificial issues. As such, they had little influence on King Mahendra's assessment of the political situation or his attitude toward the Nepali Congress government. Of a quite different nature was the demonstration in Kathmandu on December 3 in which a large crowd, consisting mostly of non-Ranas who had attained prestige and wealth under the Rana regime, gathered at the gates of the royal palace to protest against the imposition of taxes on urban land, water taps, and houses. This demonstration, which was not the work of opposition parties, set the pattern for subsequent non-party political agitation which sought King Mahendra's direct intervention in the affairs of government.

These demonstrations may have aroused the first serious doubts in King Mahendra's mind as to the appropriateness of his strictly constitutional role. In any case, from this time on the King was more inclined to pass judgements, in public, on the activities and policies of the government. The first indication of this change in attitude came at the conclusion of his tour of western Nepal in January, 1960. On previous occasions the King had used his tours to redress local grievances by settling lawsuits, bestowing favours, and making liberal donations to local institutions. Upon the inauguration of an elected government, some aspects of the royal tours had become redundant, if not irrelevant. Nevertheless, the King's tour of western Nepal in the winter of 1959/60 was carried out along the same lines as his earlier tours and, as such, constituted a minor breach of his status as a constitutional monarch.

Even more significant was the speech the King gave at a public reception at Nepalganj on January 30 upon the conclusion of the tour. He remarked:

> ...the people should direct the elected government on the right path. If the people fail to do so and corruption continues to increase in the country, we shall have to take another step to fulfil our duty...Democracy was ushered into our country and the last elections were held with the cooperation of all the people for the achievement of these objectives. If democracy fails to achieve these things, it is meaningless. It is of no use if it brings harm to the people, discourages industrialization, makes administration of justice more costly and difficult, encourages bribery and corruption, increases the rate of unemployment, makes persons in the government see only their own selfish interests, and gives antinational elements the opportunity to take undue advantage. The responsibility to see that these things do not happen, along with the responsibility to protect their freedom, has also devolved on the Nepali people. Every Nepali citizen should work with the full realization of this responsibility so that I may not adopt another measure to fulfill my responsibility. Here I would also like to say that I, too, have some duties—these are to safeguard the sovereignty and independence of the country and to look aftet such works as are conducive to national welfare. If hindrances really come in the way, I am prepared to do whatever is the need of the hour. What I want is that I should always get the cooperation of the people, as ever.

Although King Mahendra did not refer to the Nepali Congress government specifically, it was obvious that his comments constituted an appraisal of its record to date. What led to this outburst on the part of a monarch who had a reputation for deliberateness and caution is a matter for conjecture. Most of his hypothetically stated accusations had a strong contemporary ring to them, for these were precisely what critics of the government were saying. By repeating their complaints King Mahendra lent the prestige of his high office to their views and a degree of substantiation to the opposition's case. It can hardly have been strictly coincidental that opposition elements grew more demonstrative, vociferous, and obstreperous subsequently.

The royal message issued on the occasion of "National Day." February 18, also contained a veiled criticism of the Nepali Congress government. In what was in effect an exhortation to the government, King Mahendra remarked:

> If, discarding anarchism and narrow-mindedness, the government gives priority to the welfare of the country—only then can the people understand the policies of the government.

King Mahendra returned to the theme of need for better rapport between the government and the people during a speech at Rajbiraj on March 12 to mark the unveiling of a statue of the late King Tribhuwan:

> All must have realized that those who are actively engaged in nation building tasks must understand the situation in the country. If we work without understanding this, all our labour will be fruitless and both the people and the government will be blamed. Therefore it has become essential that responsible persons should think twice before starting any work. Without resources no work can be started. It is the duty of the government to start a planned economy and it is also the duty of the people to take part in the national development programme.

One feature of the King's critical remarks should be noticed, although perhaps its political import is not completely obvious. On both occasions when the King delivered highly political speeches at Nepalganj and Rajbiraj, the Prime Minister was out of the country, on the former occasion in India and on the latter in China.

When Parliament reconvened on April 1, King Mahendra delivered from the throne an address prepared by the Cabinet in which he cataloged exhaustively—perhaps monotonously—all the principal accomplishments of the government in the past year. About one week later, he left on state visits to Japan, the United States and Canada which kept him away from Nepal for more than three months. A Regency Council under the chairmanship of his brother, Prince Himalaya, was appointed to act on his behalf in his absence. In a message issued on the eve of his departure, he defined the spheres of responsibility of the Cabinent, the Regency Council, and the people:

> The Cabinet is there to establish peace and order, expedite reconstruction works, and carry out the day to day administration of the country. We have formed a Regency Council under the leadership of my brother, His Royal Highness Prince Himalaya Vir Vikram Shah Deva, to discharge functions on our behalf during our absence. There is no dobut that, if all the people of the country identify their interests and welfare with that of the whole nation and maintain a liberal and broad outlook, we shall always be accorded an honoured seat in the comity of nations, and we shall achieve much progress in every walk of life.

But on the day before the King was to leave the country on his extensive world tour, he was intercepted by refugees from West No. 1 while returning from inaugurating a water filtration plant at Balaju. The demonstrators asked the King to intervene directly to improve law and order in their district, and the King was reported to have assured them that necessary measures would soon be adopted to that effect. This incident, even if deliberately timed by the refugees to coincide with the King's departure, presaged an ominous domestic situation during his prolonged absence.

King Mahendra left Kathmandu on April 10, accompanied by a large personal and official retinue, including Deputy Prime Minister Suvarna Shamsher. At the conclusion of his state visit to Japan (April 18-25), the King and his entourage flew to the United States at the invitation of the government. During this trip, he had an apportunity to express his opinions upon the political system in Nepal in particular and world affairs in general. In his address to the United States Congress on April 28 he observed:

> You are all familiar with the strains and difficulties under which all newly established democracies have to work... Provision for fully representative institutions of government and legislatures, respect for fundamental rights and due process of law, respect for freedom and dignity of the individual are some of the basic principles that underlie our constitution. As is apparent to you, the constitution of Nepal is based on the concepts of law, liberty, and rights prevalent for a long time in your own country.
>
> ...We believe in an independent foreign policy of jugding every international issue on its merits without consideration of anybody's fear or favour and in a policy of non-entanglement...This may sound a little idealistic and a little too impractical but as a small nation we feel that is the best way in which we can contribute to the discussions and deliberations in the United Nations and to the interests of world peace and friendly relations among them.

Addressing the National Press Club in Washington on April 29, he remarked:

> Nepal's is a test case as to whether a small country situated between two big countries [India and China] can, in the realities of power relations in the mid-twentieth century world, preserve its independence, freedom and sovereignty in its own way and manner. On the answer to this question will depend the life and future of the principles of international justice and the ideas of co-existence of big and small nations.

In a speech at a dinner given by the Far East American Council of Commerce and Industry in New York on May 2, King Mahendra invited American businessmen to invest in Nepal and promised them the fullest possible scope for private enterprise. Then he went on to observe that the standard of living in Nepal was one of the lowest in the world, and that if democracy was to survive in that country, it must be able to deliver the goods as quickly as possible.

Speaking at a dinner in Los Angeles on May 10, King Mahendra pointed out that the practice of peaceful coexistence had preserved the independence of Nepal for more than three thousand years. The Nepali Ambassador to the United States, Rishikesh Shah, elaborated King Mahendra's point and offered the "unblemished integrity of Nepal as a model for the practice of peaceful co-existence by nations of different ideologies."

King Mahendra began his state visit to Canada on May 25. On the following day he held a press conference in Montreal and observed that Nepal's relations with Communist China were strictly formal and cordial. Referring to the political situation in Nepal, he said that Nepali Communists had been thwarted by the eighteen-month-old democratic Constitution: "Wherever the communists are not banned but are allowed to work openly, they have made slow progress"—an interesting comment in view of his later banning of the Communist party (and all other parties) in December, 1960.

After completing his official visits, King Mahendra left for Nepal on June 16, with visits to Lisbon, Paris, Frankfurt, Vienna, Tehran, Kabul, Srinagar, and New Delhi on the way, and arrived in Kathmandu on July 28. Once again the West No. 1 refugees intercepted the Kings procession on the road, demanding the formation of a Royal Commission to investigate their grievances. King Mahendra replied at a public reception:

> Upon reaching India, I learnt that disturbances were still continuing in West No. 1 near the capital. If true, this is highly distressing, but I hope that with one year of experience in running the administration, the government must have paid proper attention to it.

Turning to the Chinese incursion into Nepali territory in June, he commented:

> The highly unfortunate incident that took place last month on our northern borders had naturally wounded the feelings

> of the people of Nepal. I am however fully confident that such a mistake will never be repeated by our friendly neighbour. Mere talk is never effective in achieving the progress of the country. In the modern world the wise course is to move patiently according to the time.

Soon after King Mahendra's return, opposition elements—no doubt, taking comfort from the implied criticisms of the government in the royal statements—intensified their agitational activities. Refugees from West No. 1 continued to demonstrate stubbornly for restitution of their lost property and maintenance of law and order in their distrtct. The King, in order to apprise himself fully of the situation in the country, began a series of interviews with members of the Cabinet and with opposition leaders. He met with the entire Cabinet on August 6 and, reportedly, demanded information on the progress of the government's activities. Consequently, the month of August was filled with rumours that the King planned to dismiss the Nepali Congress government because of its shortcomings B.P. Koirala's allegedly critical remarks about the Constitution at the Nepali Congress party conference in May were widely publicized, and the so-called lack of harmony between the King and the Cabinet was soon described as a personal struggle between King Mahendra, who upheld the Constitution as it was, and B.P. Koirala, who wanted to amend it. Indeed, one of the local weeklies reported that the King had succumbed to Cabinet pressure and had advised the Prime Minister to amend the Constitution if it had any undemocratic features.

While all these ominous remours were circulating in August, Tulsi Giri resigned from the Cabinet. The reported tension between the King and the Cabinet dtd not express itself in any conspicuous form, but King Mahendra continued to play an assertive and political role in dealing with opposition groups and individuals. In his reply to the organizers of the Jana Hit Sangha, who had petitioned the King to repeal the government's taxation and land reform measures, he observed:

> It is not proper for His Majesty to intervene in any way from time to time. If you think that the government whom

> you chose has acted in a way detrimental to the interests of the country or any of its citizens, every Nepali citizen has the right to express his opposition according to rules. If, therefore, with the welfare of the people and the country in mind, you initiate any good step in a democratic manner. His Majesty the King will definitely act for the equal protection and welfare of nationalism, the country, and the people.

In the circumstances, this statement was a virtual incitement to the Jana Hit Sangha to continue its agitation, which was aimed specifically at the dismissal of the Nepali Congress Cabinet and the reinstitution of a direct-rule system.

On October 17, the King and the Queen, accompanied by a retinue including Deputy Prime Minister Suvarna Shamsher, arrived in London to begin a three-day state visit, the first ever made there by a Nepali monarch. Having completed the state visit, King Mahendra stayed on for an additional two weeks, inspecting educational establishments and industrial plants throughout the United Kingdom. He returned to Kathmandu on November 9. During his absence the police firing in Gorkha had occurred, resulting in the reported loss of seven lives. In his reply to the civic reception held for him at the Kathmandu airport, King Mahendra commented:

> Like other patriots, we have been exceedingly grieved to hear that during our absence, unfortunately, disturbances occurred in some parts of the country and some people were killed. But I have nothing to say further on this matter without understanding the facts property. We are fully confident that by the grace of God and with the efforts of patriots, law and order will be maintained all over the country and our country will go on marching along the path of progress.

November 11 was the tenth anniversary of the 1950 revolution. The Nepali Congress government decided to commemorate the occasion by inaugurating development projects all over Nepal, estimated to cost more than 100 million rupees, as part of the government's effort to spend the largely unused allocation of the first Five-Year Plan by the end of the fiscal year. King Mahendra took part in some of the inauguration ceremonies, but members of the Cabinet, including Prime Minister Koirala, were far more active and enthusiastic. The King did take this opportunity to issue a message to the people:

> The world is always changing, and we feel therefore that revolution is always continuous among men. With this truth in mind, responsible persons should renounce their selfish interests and work honestly for the welfare of all or else they will be regarded as having fulfilled their selfish interests with the blood of brave persons. We therefore pray to Lord Pashupatinath that he should kindle the true revolution in the minds of all the people of Nepal to enable them to remain honest, renounce selfish interests and mutual quarrels, and devote themselves to service.

Viewed after the event, this message may well seem to have been intended to prepare the ground for the royal *coup d'etat* that came five weeks later.

The December, 1960, Coup

The Indian Commander in Chief, General Thimayya, arrived in Kathmandu on December 8, 1960, for a one-week official visit. Deputy Prime Minister Suvarna Shamsher left for Calcutta on December 12—for personal reasons. The much-publicized Nepali Youth Conference, attended by a number of delegates from foreign countries, began its session on the morning of December 15. By evening of that fateful day, all the members of the Nepali Congress Cabinet that were in Kathmandu had been arrested, and King Mahendra had sounded the death knell of parliamentary democracy in a broadcast to the country over Radio Nepal.

The Royal Proclamation leveled several specific charges against the Nepali Congress government, alleging that the elected government had (a) set aside the interests of the country and the people and wielded authority in a manner designed solely to advance party interests; (b) attempted to dislocate and paralyze the administrative machinery in contravention of the laws of the realm; (c) encouraged corrupt practices; (d) proved incapable of maintaining law and order; (e) produced a disturbed and vitiated atmosphere by pursuing impractical measures; (f) encouraged antinational elements. With some slight verval modifications, these vague allegations have been endlessly repeated in government pronouncements and the local press, but have never been substantiated by documentation or appropriate proceedings in any court of law.

Before commencing a discussion of the new political system which King Mahendra has introduced, it would be useful to analyze his apparent motives in discarding parliamentary democracy and also the situation in Nepal which permitted him to take such drastic action with impunity. Only briefly noted in the world press other than in India, these dramatic events were widely interpreted abroad as falling within the same general pattern as similar developments in Pakistan, Indonesia, Burma, Turkey, Iraq and Korea in which Western-style parliamentary institutions had been abolished because of their alleged unsuitability or failure. King Mahendra has himself advanced such an interpretation of the December, 1960 *coup* as, in a sense, justifying and legitimatizing his action.

How valid is this interpretation of these events in Nepal? There is, undoubtedly, a superficial similarity between the December *coup* in Nepal and developments in other Asian countries. On closer observation, however, it is also clear that there were crucial and basic differences which distinguished the Nepal situation. Probably the most important was the relatively minor part played by the military in the royal *coup*—a striking contrast to the situation in Pakistan, Burma, Korea, and Turkey, where military men dominated what were essentially revolutionary movements. There was no "Young Turk" faction in the Nepal state army with pronounced political views and ambitions, demanding and forcing changes in the country's political structure. Indeed, the military establishment has been remarkably quiescent in Nepal in recent years. To the extent that it did play a role in the December *coup*, it functioned as an instrument of the King.

A second feature that distinguished the December *coup* in Nepal from superficially similar developments elsewhere in Asia and Africa was its essentially conservative character. What the *coup* really signified, at least initially, was the restoration of the essential characteristics of the political system as these existed up to the inauguration of parliamentary democracy in 1959. The *coup* had none of the momentum or *esprit de corps* which marked similar developments elsewhere in Asia, nor did it consolidate the position of a new ruling elite. On the contrary, the dominant political and social forces in the new structure were and are the same traditional social and economic groups that the King had depended on before the 1959 general elections.

Never openly discussed, but certainly one of the most vital considerations leading to the abrogation of parliamentary institutions, was King Mahendra's dissatisfaction with the relegation of the Crown to a comparatively minor role in the governmental structure after the installation of the Nepali Congress government. Another factor may have been King Mahendra's suspicion that the "socialist-oriented" Nepali Congress leaders were plotting the eventual abolition of the monarchy. Certain indiscreet remarks by Nepali Congress leaders alluding to the allegedly obstructionist role played by the King and the 1959 Constitution seemed to add substance to the King's apprehensions. Leaders of other political parties and a few disaffected Nepali Congress leaders were only too ready to caution the King about the Nepali Congress's ultimate intentions. In any case, such warnings could count on a receptive audience.

Whether there was any substance to King Mahendra's suspicion that the Nepali Congress government was plotting the overthrow of the monarchy is questionable. The Nepali

Congress was predominately a young intellectuals' party and, like most young Nepali intellectuals, was prone to view monarchical institutions as unmodern and, hence, dispensable. But B. P. Koirala and the top echelons of the party seem to have been concerned more with minimizing possible sources of conflict with the King than with plotting his downfall. That the Cabinet would have deliberately instigated a constitutional crisis under the prevailing conditions is unlikely; rather, it would have preferred to leave the question of the ultimate fate of the monarchy to the distant future when a more objective evaluation of its role in the parliamentary system would be feasible.

This does not mean, of course, that a constitutional crisis over the monarchy was not intrinsic to the trend of political developments. There was, indeed, a fundamental difference between the King and the Nepali Congress over the proper role of the monarchy in contemporary Nepal. Since ascending the throne in 1955, King Mahendra has consistently stressed the theory that the monarchy is essential to orderly progress and to the very existence of Nepal as a nation. In this view, the Crown is the only institution capable of providing strong national leadership. It is, therefore, the responsibility of the King to function in the political sphere, directly and decisively when necessary, and as the ultimate source of authority in less critical situations.

While the Nepali Congress has always publicly conceded the central role played by the monarchy, it has also insisted that the Crown can serve in this capacity only as long as it functions constitutionally—*i.e.*, the King should reign but not rule—and that the Crown's role as the symbol of national unity is contingent upon the King's acting as a unifying and nationalizing influence. In contrast, the Nepali Congress has charged King Mahendra with frequently playing upon factionalism within the parties to disrupt them and divide them in order to further his own narrow political goals. Whether he actively instigated the schisms and factional division in the parties, as is alleged, or merely took advantage of their existence is incidental to the question. The effect would have been equally injurious in either case for it, by encouraging instability in the party system and, indirectly, in the administration as well, The Crown, according to the Nepali Congress leaders, should remain above politics, not indulge in them.

Another factor that might have precipitated the King's intervention was his reading of the changing line-up of political forces in the country in 1960. Political observers had sensed the need for a strong opposition party to act as a countervailing force to the Nepali Congress government ever since its formation. There was wide expectation at the time that the Gorkha Parishad leadership would attempt to rally all the anti-Nepali Congress political elements and present a strong opposition to the government. This, however, failed to materialize; instead, the Gorkha Parishad under the leadership of Bharat Shamsher was moving closer to a coalition with the Nepali Congress. It was obvious that a working coalition between these two parties would result in the establishment of a monolithic party government, the extinction of all democratic opposition, and the emergence of the Communist party as the only political alternative to the Nepali Congress's democratic-socialist programme. And, more importantly, if the situation had developed along these lines, King Mahendra would have found it extremely difficult to turn down a proposal for a national Cabinet. He would have been caught in the awkward situation of wanting a faster pace of economic development but not at the risk of perpetuating a Nepali Congress—Gorkha Parishad political monopoly in the country.

But it is doubtful that King Mahendra's deep-seated aversion to political parties and party politics would long permit him to play a purely constitutional role, as designated in the 1959 constitutional system. Several of the King's statements, some dating as early as 1951, were caustic in their appraisal of party leaders and frankly skeptical of the capacity of the parties to provide the kind of vigorous, honest political leadership Nepal has needed and has seldom had. In banning the parties after the December *coup*, the King was not only ridding himself of irritating critics and potentially dangerous rivals for power, but was also, in his view, eliminating a pernicious influence upon the body politic in Nepal. A broader, more tolerant and comprehensive perspective of the role played by parties in any democratic political system has never impressed itself upon the King.

Sources of Support for the Royal Coup

Any analysis of King Mahendra's motivations in dismissing the Nepali Congress must necessarily be confined to the realm of mere speculation, for the King has not chosen to speak frankly on this subject as yet. It is possible, however, to explain how it was possible for him, with such little difficulty, to carry out a *coup* against a government that had won a decisive electoral victory twenty months earlier. The answer is that important and articulate groups upon which the King could depend for support were organized and capable of action, while the elements in Nepali society which supported the Nepali Congress were not nearly so well organized or influential.

A large majority of the landowning and commercial interests in Nepal, for instance, were unalterably opposed to the Nepali Congress government's land and taxation policy. The moderate character of the economic legislation enacted by the Koirala Cabinet did not diminish their apprehension, since these measures were considered to be merely the first in a series of gradually more drastic changes in the land and taxation system. These vested interest groups, with their close ties to various cliques in the palace, had long since concluded that the King was the last effective barrier to the imposition of fundamental economic reforms, and this attitude was crucial in determining their response to the December *coup*.

A small but influential conglomeration of tradition-oriented groups provided the core for another center of resistance to the Nepali Congress regime. Fiercely monarchist in outlook and deeply disturbed by the progressive diminution of the role and powers of the King, they were appalled by the secular, "socialist" aspects of the Koirala government. Orthodox Hindus for the most part, they viewed the refusal of post-1951 governments to apply the dharmashastric clauses (*i.e.*, caste provisions) that the Rana regime had made an integral part of the Nepali legal code as subversive to the principles upon which Nepal's society was based. The monarchy was considered to be the last important obstacle to invidious influences from the outside world, particularly India. Anything that bolstered the throne was assured of their support. This attitude was strengthened by King Mahendra's own traditional Hindu predilections which were reflected in the clauses in both the 1959 and the 1962 Constitutions that barred ascent to the throne to anyone but an "adherent of Aryan culture and Hindu region."

The allegedly "pro-India" tendencies of the Nepali Congress's foreign policy aroused the opposition of several other groups that differed basically from those so far discussed. These were, in essence, "anti-India and pro-China" in orientation, though for widely varied reasons. Included within this category were the Communities, some students and young intellectuals incensed over what they interpreted as Indian interference in Nepal's internal politics, renascent Buddhist groups resentful of the infliction of "Brahmanic" social regulations on non-Hindu elements of Nepal's society, and even some reformist, modernist groups that strongly opposed the anti-egalitarian features of the caste system, whose presence in Nepal they attributed to age-old influences from India.

Many members of these groups are not pro-Communist in any real sense, and even their ostensibly pro-China attitudes seem to be a thin veneer assumed for the occasion. They are, however, suspicious and resentful of India and are susceptible to anti-Indian slogans, even when used to disguise attacks on policies and institutions they would otherwise be inclined to support. It is on this single issue, moreover, that much of the educated youth of Nepal and King Mahendra can find common ground, for in most other respects their views are widely divergent.

King Mahendra has also drawn considerable support from some elements in the bureaucracy, in particular the royal palace secretariat and some old-line. Rana-trained officials in the government secretariat who lost much of their power and influence through the installation of parliamentary institutions. Both these groups strongly supported the reestablishment of the pre-1959 governmental system under which they had flourished and, moreover, were well situated to influence King Mahendra in this direction.

Probably the most important mainstay of the King, however, is the support he has received from the army. This support was particularly crucial in the immediate post-*coup* period. Not only did it provide the King with the physical capacity to suppress disturbances, but it gave him another source from which reliable appointments could be made to the Central Secretariat and other government posts. A number of army officers were appointed to high positions in the civil administration immediately after the *coup*, replacing public servants suspected of too close ties with the Nepali Congress regime.

That the military has been so docile and easily managed is rather astonishing in Nepal, where the army leadership has had a long tradition of direct and open intervention in politics, going back at least to the days when the country was first unified under the Shah dynasty in the latter part of the eighteenth century. An apolitical military leadership has been the exception rather than the rule in Nepal's history, and the existing situation is largely a tribute to King Mahendra's perceptive and careful planning. Fully cognizant of the role played by the army in mid-nineteenth-century developments which deprived the ruling dynasty of all but nominal sovereign powers, King Mahendra has taken care to emasculate the military as a potent political force—and with considerable success.

To accomplish this end, King Mahendra has utilized various tactics. He has been extremely careful, for instance, to retain complete and direct authority over the military in his capacity as Supreme Commander in Chief. The Defence Ministry at the

Central Secretariat has had little influence in military affairs except insofar as it functioned as an instrument of the royal palace. Up to May, 1959, King Mahendra always selected as Defence Minister someone closely connected with the royal family, even when a party Cabinet was in office.

The Nepali Congress Cabinet was the first in which a party member held the Defence portfolio. Nevertheless, the King was careful to retain ultimate and direct authority over the army. Prime Minister Koirala, who also held the Defence portfolio, was probably less involved in Defence Ministry affairs than his predecessors had been. In any case, the King faced no difficulty with the Defence Ministry when he utilized the state army in the course of the December *coup*.

King Mahendra has also paid close attention to the composition of the officer corps since coming to the throne. It has been reported that he has sometimes barred promotion to ambitious young officers suspected of political motivations or interests in favour of men who were more dependable politically. Whether intentionally or not, the officer crops has been remarkably apolitical since 1956, when the King nipped a potentially dangerous plot in which several lower-level officers were involved.

A somewhat less obvious source of support for the December *coup* was provided by opposition party leaders. With relatively few exceptions, most of the opposition leaders welcomed the King's action and promised their cooperation in the establishment of a new political structure. In view of the ban placed on all political parties shortly afterward, and the King's announced intention to dispense with parliamentary government based upon the party system, this attitude would seem to have had masochistic overtones. On closer examination, however, it can be seen that only a few of the opposition party leaders had really benefitted from the inauguration of the parliamentary system or held expectations of doing so in the future: the overwhelming victory of the Nepali Congress in the 1959 elections had deprived most of them and their parties of any real influence in Nepali politics.

In these circumstances many opposition politicians had become increasingly unhappy with the parliamentary system, which had proved so ill-suited for the proper appreciation of their talents. Few of them were prepared to undertake the hard task of building a mass-support party from the bottom up, and their only hope for regaining political influence was through royal rather than popular support. These politicians were not particularly distressed with King Mahendra's decision to replace parliamentary institutions with another variation of a direct-rule system under which political advancement would depend primarily on the patronage of the King. Under this system anybody could become a Minister, without reference to the extent of popular support he might enjoy.

Concluding Remarks

The royal *coup* of December, 1960, will undoubtedly go down in the history of Nepal as an important landmark in the evolution of the political relationship between the Shah rulers and their Prime Ministers. During the pre-Rana period this relationship had been marked by considerable violence and tension. Indeed, until the emergence of Jang Bahadur Rana the careers of Nepal Prime Ministers had ended usually in political disgrace and frequently in violent death. After the establishment of the Rana regime, the Shah monarchy was reduced to a status of political nonentity for a century. The political restoration of the as a primary objective of his regime. But there are no indications as yet that panchayats and class organizations are less susceptible to regional, parochial, and other narrow interests or are more "national" in perspective than political parties. Indeed, they lack one essential criterion of the party system that was important in this respect: namely, the necessity for parties to make some form of appeal on the national level to have any hope of success in elections. The dynamics of panchayat politics seems to have created a situation in which personality, rather than programme, is the decisive factor and at the same time to have blocked most of the channels through which political leaders gained satisfaction in the past. This has certainly been the case with regard to the Council of Ministers since December, 1960, and few would argue that the results have been encouraging. Whether in the end these conditions foster national unity or national frustration is debatable.

3

Panchayat Raj and Political Development

The speed and efficiency with which the December *coup* was carried out prevented the organization of effective opposition from any quarter. Having come to expect more subtlety and indirection from King Mahendra, the party leaders were stunned by the King's action and it was several weeks before they were able to recover their composure. Their reaction to the total ban imposed on political activity ranged from sullen compliance to a rather smug and expectant acquiescence. Many party leaders issued statements publicly supporting the King, although in some cases only as the price for release from prison or to avoid imprisonment. It was obvious from the enthusiasm with which most of the opposition party leaders greeted the overthrow of the Nepali Congress government and the termination of the parliamentary system that they viewed the *coup* as an unprecedented opportunity to improve their own and, as a secondary consideration, their party's position.

The immediate consequences of the December *coup* were, of course, particularly disastrous for the Nepali Congress, which lost most of its top leadership through imprisonment, exile, or desertion. With only a few exceptions, all the Congress leaders in Nepal either suffered imprisonment or pledged their loyalty to the royal regime. Among this latter group were several who were activity participating in the government; a larger group promised to abstain from political activity in a exchange for their freedom. The purge of Nepali Congress workers was carried out with considerable thoroughness, even on the district level. Local party organizations were disbanded and the party workers either imprisoned or dispersed if they exhibited any disinclination to cooperate with the new regime. At all levels, government officials appointed by the Koirala Cabinet or suspected of too close ties with the Nepali Congress were arbitrarily dismissed, often in direct contravention of Nepal's public service regulations.

A few influential Nepali Congress leaders were either in India at the time of the *coup* or else made their way across the border subsequently. Indeed, the first public expression of opposition to the *coup* came during a convention held by approximately 150 political workers from the central Terai district of Birganj, who met in Raxaul (Bihar) in mid-January, 1961. Shortly thereafter, several hundred Nepali Congress leaders and workers held an emergency secret convention in Patna (Bihar), which was also attended by several leaders from other Nepali political parties. The resolutions publicly adopted by the convention were comparatively mild in tone, merely petitioning the King to reconvene Parliament and release political prisoners. According to the party's general secretary, however, this convention secretly "laid down the line of action, and decided to protest against the King's autocratic regime and build a resistance movement."

It was fairly obvious, however, that the Nepali Congress was in no position at this time to launch a major movement against the King, nor was the mood of the country such as to provide much encouragement about the results if one should be attempted. The Congress had virtually disappeared as an effective political organization, and it was only gradually that an underground organization was built, concentrated in the Terai and the far western and far eastern hill areas where Kathmandu's writ has traditionally been tenuous.

There seem to have been some differences of opinion within the Nepali Congress on the objectives of a resistance movement. A moderate faction, led by Suvarna Shamsher, had limited political goals in view, at least as far as the immediate situation was concerned. While the restoration of parliamentary democracy was the ultimate objective, the moderates were obviously prepared to accomplish this in gradual stages if the King could be persuaded to make a few concessions in this direction—*e.g.*, the release of political prisoners and the legalization of political parties. There was a more radical wing in the Nepali Congress-in-exile, however, which grew increasingly influential once it became evident that a compromise settlement with the King would not be easily achieved. This faction insisted that the party should concentrate on preparation for a full-scale armed revolt aimed at the deposition of King Mahendra and, if necessary, the abolition of the monarchical system itself. A revolutionary situation was developing in Nepal, it was argued, and the Nepali Congress must provide leadership for this movement or else see it pass under the control of the Communists.

The relative strength of the more radical wing in the Nepali Congress increased as the ranks of the party were swelled by refugees from Nepal and leaders from other political parties. As the moderates grew increasingly frustrated with their lack of success in opening negotiaitons with the King, the trend toward extreme solutions became more pronounced. One of the consequences was a series of armed attacks on government installations in the hill areas and the Terai in the late fall of 1961. These tactics presumably represented a compromise between the policies advocated by the moderate and radical factions of the Congress. From their very nature, the attacks had limited objectives and were not intended as the prelude to full-scale revolution. The Congress leaders may have hoped that a demonstration of the party's capacity to stage armed uprisings would intimidate the King and win concessions from him. In this way, the demands for action from the more radical wing of the party could be satisfied, while at the same time the moderate leadership could disown responsibility for the incidents—which were attributed to spontaneous outbursts on the part of the people—thus leaving themselves free to open negotiations with the palace if circumstances should permit.

The King demonstrated no tendency to panic or even to retreat before these tactics, which he correctly appraised as indicative of weakness rather than strength. The royal regime was frankly skeptical of the Congress party's capacity to mount any movement—nonviolent or revolutionary—that could seriously threaten the stability of the government. The policy of the government at the time of the outbreak of the Nepali Congress-inspired uprisings in the fall of 1961 was an intriguing display of politics at its pragmatic best. The government first denied that the incidents had any political significance, attributing them to the maraudings of "dacoit" (bandit) gangs. When the attracks continued and became more obviously political in character, the government completely reversed its position. Suddenly, it was admitted that the uprisings were politically motivated, allegedly the work of "antinational" elements based in India. An anti-Indian propaganda campaign was launched, obviously officially inspired, in which the Indian government was accused of interfering in Nepal's internal affairs by permitting Nepali political refugees to organize and, in some cases, launch attacks on Nepal from Indian soil.

Aside from the question of their authenticity, there can be little doubt that the allegations of Indian interference in Nepal served both the external and the domestic political objectives of the King. The anti-Indian campaign was useful, for instance, in solidifying some degree of popular support behind the regime and in stigmatizing the opposition as puppets of New Delhi intent on reimposing India's dominant influence in Nepal. The King's eager overtures to Peking, which were reaching a crucial stage in the late fall of 1961, were also justified in part on the grounds that the Indian "threat" necessitated closer relations with China. Kathmandu may also have hoped that New Delhi, alarmed by developments along its entire northern frontier, might be moved to grant concessions to Nepal with regard both to political affairs and to the Indian economic aid programme.

In spite of or perhaps because of all this maneuvering and posturing by the Nepal government, the scope and intensity of the Nepali Congress campaign increased gradually in the first half of 1962 until by summer there were few areas of the country, except within the immediate periphery of Kathmandu Valley or the more isolated sections of the northern border, that had not witnessed some manifestation of resistance to the royal regime. Most of these were localized affairs of brief duration that never seriously threatened the government's authority yet did place a tremendous strain on both the administration and the military. The steady deterioration in Nepal-India relations during this period, largely owing to the Kathmandu government's suspicion that India was secretly instigating and supporting the rebels, added to the situation a facet with far more dangerous potentialities. The royal regime rather frantically sought a way to get out of the dilemma without compromising its assiduously cultivated "nationalist" posture.

Developments outside Nepal finally permitted the royal regime to emerge from this critical situation intact and, indeed, with its prestige and authority enhanced. The Chinese incursions along the western and eastern extremities of the Sino-Indian border in October, 1962, had an immediate and dramatic impact upon the internal political situation in Nepal. On November 8, Suvarna Shamsher "suspended" the movement, reportedly on the advice of the Indian government, and one month later the campaign was formally terminated.

With these dramatic new developments came some speculation that the King and the Nepali Congress would seek an accommodation under which Suvarna Shamsher and his colleagues would accept Panchayat Raj in its essentials and would, in exchange, be permitted to return to Nepal without endangering their personal freedom. King Mahendra's "private visit" to

Calcutta in January, 1963, was rumoured to have been mativated by his decision to meet Suvarna Shamsher without the publicity that would have accompanied talks in Kathmandu. But, if reports are correct, the King did not meet Suvarna in Calcutta on that occasion or elsewhere during his tour of India one month later.

Indeed, the subsequent course of events would seem to indicate that the King either lacked interest in or was not inclined toward a settlement with the then much-truncated Nepali Congress. In the April, 1963, recognization of the government every Minister or Assistant Minister who had been advocating a moderate domestic and foreign policy was excluded. The King's position was demonstrated even more graphically in the decision of the Kathmandu special court that same month, which sentenced Suvarna Shamsher and several colleagues *in absentia* to life imprisonment on the charge of having instigated the transportation of explosive materials to Nepal for subversive purposes. It was assumed that the King would not have permitted this trial to continue or such a rigorous sentence to be imposed if he had been at all interested in a compromise settlement with the Congress. And, indeed, such an accommodation may have seemed unnecessary. The failure of direct action to achieve any positive political gains seriously undermined the Nepali Congress within Nepal and, presumably, among some of its partisans in India. There was, moreover, a broad reconciliation between New Delhi and Kathmandu in 1963 which went far to relieve the King's apprehensions that India might support or encourage forces opposed to the regime.

Nevertheless, most political observers in Nepal would admit that a *rapprochement* between the King and the Nepali Congress is the *sine qua non* for long-term political stability. There have been several attempts to bring the two antagonists together, but these have all proved abortive. The terms of settlement and, perhaps of even greater importance, the manner of the negotiating, have proven to be serious obstacles. The rather clumsy attempts by the Nepali Congress to intimidate the King into basic concessions through the incitement of sporadic violence backfired disastrously; they seem to have strengthened the King's determination to seek a solution on his own terms. Mahendra's view of his own role in Nepali history as the protector and expander of Nepal's national integrity may be of particular significance in this respect. Speculation in the sphere of personality assessment must be tenuous at best, but it is hardly probable that overt intimidation tactics would prove successful against the King—unless, of course, these were supported by an irresistible display of force. The obvious inadequacies of the Congress's revolutionary capacity, combined with its tendency to depend upon Indian influence at Kathmandu for support of its cause, were not well-conceived tactics if the object was to induce the King to agree to a compromise.

The policy pursued by the Congress has had unfortunate consequences, since it would seem that otherwise the points at issue between the King and the party were not incapable of compromise. The debate between the relative merits of parliamentary democracy and Panchayat Raj has an academic air about it, particularly in prevailing conditions. Or perhaps it would be more accurate to say that the King could define Panchayat Raj in such a way as to make it acceptable to most adherents of parliamentary democracy without seriously subverting his own political objectives. The ban on political parties and the stringent restrictions on "fundamental rights" have proved more difficult to negotiate, but the King has usually maintained that these policies would be modified if and when circumstances permitted. How the parties might be fitted into a panchayat system based on indirect elections has never been discussed, but perhaps experiences in India's Panchayat Raj and Pakistan's "Basic Democracy" system, in which elections to the lowest-level bodies are nonpartisan and the higher-level elections are fought on party and partisan lines, may prove instructive. There is, moreover, a general tendency among most Nepali political leaders to accept the fact that the King will continue to play a central role in the governmental system. Indeed, a satisfactory redefinition of "constitutional monarchy" would not seem a major problem if both sides were intent upon reaching an agreement.

Perhaps the question that has most obstructed a settlement has concerned the position of the Nepali Congress political prisoners—in particular, B.P. Koirala. The stature of the former Prime Minister has been enhanced, if anything, by his imprisonment, and the failure of the King to bring him to trial has raised doubts about the allegations of corruption and treason made against him. His refusal to renounce politics in exchange for freedom has also given him something of the aura of a political martyr. But here, again, recent developments indicate that this question may not be so nearly unsolvable as it once seemed. There were unverified but seemingly authoritative reports in early 1964 that the King was prepared to make concessions on this question if the Nepali Congress accepted the ban on party and political activity for the time being. A number of Nepali Congress workers on the regional level, some of whom had been imprisoned since December, 1960, were quietly released toward the end of 1963. According to these reports, the talks between the King's representative and the Nepali Congress failed over the political party ban issue; but the terms upon which these negotiations were based represented a considerable modification of those rigorously adhered to by both sides previously and a portent of some significance for the future.

The Nepal Communist Party

The other political parties in Nepal have not fared much better than the Nepali Congress since the December *coup* and have, indeed, lacked even the limited recuperative powers the Congress, owing to its nationwide organizational basis, has displayed. One possible exception is the Communist Party of Nepal. It is probable that the 1960 ban on political organizations and activity was felt to a lesser degree by the Communists than by the others. The Communists had functioned in an illegal capacity from 1952 to 1956, and thus had more experience with underground operations. Moreover, since the *coup*, the royal regime has taken much less stringent action against the Communists than against the Nepali Congress. Many Communist leaders and workers were able to continue their political activity virtually undisturbed, in striking contrast to the thoroughgoing efforts made to suppress the Nepali Congress at all levels. Thus the Communists have been provided with a considerable operational advantage over the Nepali Congress that may well prove to have significant long-range implications.

Despite these initial advantages, however, the Communists have not been able to seize full benefit from the situation, primarily because of the chronic struggle for power within the party Politburo. The first signs of a fundamental disagreement within the party leadership on the question of the December *coup* became evident in early 1961. The Communists, although as surprised by the King's action as were the other parties, seem to have recovered their poise more quickly. Few of the Communist leaders were apprehended in the general roundup of politicians that followed the *coup*. Before long, the party was operating underground in much the same fashion as it had done before 1956. At the time of the *coup*, the "moderate" leader, Keshar Jang Rayamajhi, was in Moscow. Thus, the first public reaction of the party to the King's move reflected the views of the "extremist" Kathmandu faction led by a Politburo member, Pushpa Lal Shrestha. On Debember 24, 1960, a cyclostyled press note was distributed, ostensibly in the name of the party, demanding the cessation of "military terror" and the reconvening of Parliament. By mid-January 1961, however, Rayamajhi and other moderate Communists had returned to Nepal from Russia, and the struggle for control of the party machinery began in earnest. The moderate faction was in a majority on the Central Committee and was able to gain approval for a more cautious policy toward the new royal regime. In the latter part of January the party issued another press note, this time reflecting the views of the moderate faction. While cautiously critical of the *coup* and demanding the release of political prisoners, the lifting of the ban on political activity, and restoration of fundamental rights, the note did not insist on the reconvening of the Parliament, thus implying acceptance of the new regime.

The intraparty dispute reached a crisis stage at the "secret" plenum session of the Central Committee held at Darbhanga, India, in March. The plenum was attended also by fifty-four delegates representing twenty-four district organizations of the party. In these stormy meetings, the Rayamajhi faction argued that the party's immediate objectives should be limited to the restoration of fundamental rights, the release of political prisoners, the withdrawal of the ban on political parties, and the election of a new Parliament in the near future. The Pushpa Lal faction, supported by the Kathmandu. Gorkha, and Bandipur party organizations, demanded the reconvening of the dissolved Parliament (*i e.*, the restoration of the Nepali Congress government) and, if necessary, the launching of a Communist-led movement to achieve this objective. A third, minor faction led by the Piuthan party unit demanded the election of a Constituent Assembly to draw up a new Constitution and the eventual establishment of a republican form of government. For all practical purposes, the two latter factions were aligned against the moderates.

The plenum session ended in a virtual stalemate, although the Rayamajhi faction was able to retain control of the Central Committee. Eleven of the seventeen members of the Central Committee were reported to be Rayamajhi supporters, while sex followed Pushpa Lal's leadership. The pro-Rayamajhi majority at the Darbhanga session was reduced to one, however, since three members of the Rayamajhi faction were in prison in Nepal and unable to attend, and a fourth resigned from the Central Committee during the session.

To negotiate the differences between the two factions, the plenum session appointed a joint committee to draw up a compromise party programme. This thankless task proved to be impossible, however, and the two factions continued their bitter debate over the question of the party's attitude toward the royal regime. There are some reasons for suspecting that the struggle in the party was not conducted solely on the verbal level. Presistent reports circulated in Kathmandu in July, alleging that a colleague had attempted to assassinate Rayamajhi. It was also at this time that the leader of the moderate faction was apprehended by the Kathmandu police under very curious circumstances. What exactly happened in this instance has never been clarified, but one Nepali journal with close ties to the Communists implied strongly that opposition elements in the party had betrayed Rayamajhi to the police. Equally intriguing was the government's sudden arrest of the leader of the "pro-monarchy" faction of the Nepal Communist party while the leader of the "extremist" faction was allowed to wander around Kathmandu, only indifferently disguised. Whatever the reasons may have been, the government reversed itself quickly, for scarcely one month later Rayamajhi was released from prison—and without having signed the usual declaration of loyalty to the King required of political prisoners.

Rumours of collaboration between Rayamajhi and certain members of the government circulated wildly in the Kathmandu bazaar in September when the Communist leader was given a passport and allowed to visit Moscow, ostensibly (and, possibly, actually) for medical treatment. His departure did nothing to reduce the tension in the party, however, and may have been partly responsible for bringing matters to a head. The moderates, bolstered by the return of the three members of the party's Central Committee who had been released from prison at approximately the same time as Rayamajhi, decided to issue a strong warning to the extremists. Pushpa Lal and his associates were threatened with expulsion from the party if they did not mend their ways, accept the decision to support the royal regime, and work within the existing institutional framework.

A serious clash occurred between the two factions at a party Central Committee meeting in Kathmandu, held either in late November or early December. Pushpa Lal insisted that the King's rule was "feudalistic" and had to be overthrown by any means, even revolution. The "bourgeois and reactionary" Indian government was only a slight improvement over the royal regime, Pusha Lal admitted, but in the circumstances New Delhi could be expected to favour and support "democratic forces" in their struggle to free Nepal from the King's "dictatorship." He also favoured an alliance with the Nepali Congress as the necessary prerequisite to a successful revolution. These views were unacceptable to the moderates, and Pushpa Lal and his supporters were threatened with expulsion from the party if they did not cease their "antiparty activities." Shortly thereafter, Pushpa Lal and severel colleagues fled to India in order, according to reports, to avoid detention by the authorities.

On arriving in India, Pushpa Lal made two conditional offered of cooperation to the Nepali Congress. These were welcomed by Suvarna Shamsher and his colleagues, though no outright acceptance of the proposal seems to have been made at that time. Indeed, the hard-pressed Congress leaders must have found the offer tempting, for the support of the Pushpa Lal faction would have augmented and supplemented the Nepali Congress revolutionary potential. Insignificant though they might be numerically, the supporters of the extremist faction of the Communist party were concentrated in some of the most vital areas of Nepal: Kathmandu Valley, Gorkha in the western hills, and Dharan in the lower eastern hills. These were areas in which strong Communist party organizations had existed before the December *coup* and where some residue of this structure must have survived. Even more crucial perhaps were the connections Pushpa Lal had with the Communist-dominated Peasants' Organization through one of his adherents, Tulsi Lal Amatya. Moreover, Pushpa Lal was probably in a position to solicit assistance from sections of the Communist Party of India that otherwise might have been antagonistic toward the Nepali Congress.

For nearly three months Pushpa Lal toured areas of India in which there were substantial settlements of Nepali migrants—followed very closely, it should be noted, by D P.

Adhikari, then affiliated with the moderate faction of the party. Finally, Pushpa Lal announced in early April, 1962, that a "Congress of the Communist Party of Nepal" would be held the next month. The ostensible purpose of the congress was to formulate policy; actually it was to set up what amounted to a "parallel" Communist party. The announcement brought forth an immediate denunciation from the Rayamajhi faction. Speaking on behalf of the Central Committee of the party, Kamar Sah issued a statement in Kathmandu accusing the Pushpa Lal group of "actively conspiring against the central leadership, violating the Leninist standard of party life, and indulging in factional activities to undermine the very unity of the party." Despite these "anti-party" activities, the announcement continued, the Central Committee was "confident that the rank and file of the party, educated in Lenist principles," would defeat the "nefarious designs of the Pushpa Lal group to split party unity" and that the party would "advance further in its goal to serve the people and the country in its glorious past tradition."

Kamar Sah's warnings were ignorted, and a meeting, termed an *Adhibeshan* ("general congress") of the party, was held in Banaras in mid-May, reportedly drawing representatives from eight of the thirty-five districts of Nepal. Seven resolutions were passed, the most important of which called for a revolution against the royal regime, though no date was set for the commencement of the movement. A second resolution expelled ten moderate members of the Central Committee—including Rayamajhi, Sambhu Ram Shrestha, Kamar Sah, D.P. Adhikari, and P.B. Malla—for varying periods, on charges of betraying the party by supporting the King's "antidemocratic" moves. To replace them, a new Central Committee was appointed, of whose nineteen members only four had been members of the old committee. In addition, a new National Council was formed, most of whose fifty-one members were also newcomers.

The Banaras meetings failed to result in an open alliance between the Pushpa Lal faction and the Nepali Congress, but they were effective in completing the split within the Communist Party of Nepal. In late May, the Central Committee of the party (Rayamajhi faction) issued a statement condemning the violent activities of the "antinational elements" in India:

> No Democratic movement succeeds through violence and terroristic activities. It can succeed only through a mass movement launched inside the country. Violent actions weaken the mass movement. The Communist party therefore condemns such activities.

This statement, astonishing in view of its source, would seem to be directed more at Pushpa Lal and his supporters in the party than at the Nepali Congress. By summer, all efforts to prevent the formalization of the split within the Communist party leadership had come to naught. Finally in September, the Central Committee (Rayamajhi faction) expelled Pushpa Lal, Tulsi Lal Amatya, and Hikmat Singh from the party. Other members of the party who supported these three "deviationists," it was stated, would be dealt with by the appropriate committees of the level on which they worked.

With the revolutionary path to communism discarded (only temporarily, presumably), the Rayamajhi faction adopted another familiar Communist tactic—a "united front of all democratic forces" in Nepal. One of the first indications of the new direction of Communist policy was an article in a pro-Communist weekly complaining that "no united and organized front" had yet been established to meet the challenge of the "Indian-American puppet forces led by Suvarna and Bharat. As the government's ban on party activity was a serious, possibly insurmountable obstacle to the formation of a united front, much of the Communists' persuasive talents was employed in a campaign to convince the King that the dynamics of such a movement were basically in conformity with his own political objectives.

To emphasize even further the "royalist", character of the proposed united front, the Central Committee of the Communist party suggested that the King should call a conference on this subject at the royal palace. "All nationalistic and democratic forces standing for different ideologies and policies and having a programme for the solution of national problems" should be invited, the party executive suggested. The use of the adjective "nationalistic" was particularly significant, since in current Nepali political parlance the Nepali Congress and allied "antinational" elements would automatically be excluded from the front. The term "democratic" on the other hand, is interpreted so broadly in Nepal that hardly any organization could reasonably be excluded for being undemocratic; thus any of the parties or groups representing traditional and visited interests could join at their own discretion.

The relationship between the front and the government was also a delicate question upon which the Communists attempted to reassure the King. The front would not be a political party, the Communists said, nor would it be entrusted with the task of running the government:

> Of course, it would be indispensable to maintain close contact and hold consultations between such a front and the government. Each will have to respect the other, as otherwise there will be no national unity. In case such a front is formed, it will not be able to assume the form of a "party," though its members following different ideologies and principles may work for nationalism, for the country's development, and for democracy. Instead, such a front would put an end to mutual rivalry and opposition for the sake of opposition and pave the way for a healthy competition for constructive work and service to the country.

As described so enthusiastically by the Communists, the front would be another instrument through which the government could implement its political and economic programmes.

Needless to say, there was some doubt in official and intellectual circles in Kathmandu that the Communists intended to allow the front to function in this fashion. There were, it was pointed out, several aspects of such a front that might well prove advantageous to the Communists. First, it would provide the party......an organization within which Communist cadras could operate on a legal level even while the party itself was still banned. Furthermore, the Communists would be assured easier access to such administrative institutions as the panchayats and class organizations, which they had been assiduously attempting to infiltrate. Finally, the party could use its participation in the front to seize a central and possibly dominant position among the remnants of the political party movement in Nepal, in preparation for the time when it might once again have to compete with the Nepali Congress.

The termination of the Nepali Congress-led movement in December, 1962, in the wake of Chinese aggression against India, placed the Pushpa Lal faction in a quandary. Pushpa Lal' policy had been based on the proposition that the overthrow of King Mahendra should be the primary goal of the Communist Party of Nepal, even if the immediate result was a regime dominated by the Nepali Congress. It was now obvious that this policy was unrealistic and that terroristic tactics had been unavailling. Reportedly, a number of Communist party workers in exile in India became disillusioned, returned to Nepal in 1963, and presumably made their peace with the Rayamajhi faction. Further, a serious rift had developed within the extremist faction between the followers of Pushpa Lal and Tulsi Lal Amatya, who succeeded Pushpa Lal as general secretary of the party-in exile in 1962.

How reliable these reports may be is open to question, but it was apparent, nevertheless, that the challenge to Rayamajhi's leadership was receding. The proroyalist policy of the moderate faction brought tangible political rewards, including Rayamajhi's appointment to the Raj Sabha, the appointment of a former member of the party's Central Committee as an Assistant Minister, and the election of a pro-Communist as Deputy Speaker of the National Panchayat. There are some indications, however, that Rayamajhi's "gradualist" approach has not been popular with party workers who are emotionally anti-monarchical and action-oriented. The party also seems to have lost some of the appeal it formerly had for young intellectuals, who are no longer so prone to view the Communists— at least, the domestic variety—as the wave of the future.

Besides internal factors in the divisions that have rent the Communist party, international developments such as the Sino-Indian border conflict and the Sino-Russian ideological and tactical disputes have had an important impact. There is, as yet, no coherent division of the party into pro-Soviet or pro-Chinese wings—at least, on the public level. Like most others in Asia, the Nepali Communists find it extremely embarrassing to have to make a choice between the two Communist giants. The position of the party is doubly complex because of the Sino-Indian struggle for influence throughout the Himalayan area, which has now become inextricably enmeshed in the Sino-Soviet dispute and in the division of the Indian party into nominally "pro-Soviet" and "pro-China" factions.

No top Nepali Communist leaders have openly declared themselves in the quarrels dividing the Communist world. Tulsi Lal Amatya has been accused of harbouring "pro-China" sentiment, but his position as an exile in India makes it imprudent for him to align openly with the Chinese camp. Rayamajhi's contacts have largely been with the Russians. Presumably his faction would line up with the Soviet Union if it ever became necessary to choose sides; at present it carefully maintains a neutral position and refrains from commenting publicly on any of the issues in dispute. Such discretion is by all odds the better part of valor, for there are indications that both major factions of the party would be even further divided if they had to declare themselves publicly on the Sino-Soviet rift.

Other Political Parties

The reactions of the various political parties to the Decembar *coup* was indicative of the basic malaise endemic to the political party movement in Nepal. The abject failure of most party organizations to protest—much less, challenge—the King's action constituted an eloquent commentary on the narrow, self-centered approach of many party leaders and on the lack of a strong popular base for the party movement as a whole. King Mahendra could concentrate his attention on the destruction of the one party with some national support, confident that most of the other party leaders, oblivious of the long-range implications of this policy for their own organizations, would loudly applaud. The King once again proved a shrewd appraiser of the men and organizations competing for political influence, playing upon their recurrent hopes and fears with the skill of a virtuoso.

The objects of the government's repressive actions at the time of the *coup* were not, however, limited to the Nepali Congress leaders. Most of the opposition party leaders, including Tanka Prasad Acharya and Bhadrakali Mishra of the Praja Parishad, Bharat Shamsher and Mrigendra Shamsher of the Gorkha Parishad, K. I. Singh of the United Democratic Party, D. R. Regmi of the Nepali National Congress, and Ranga Nath Sharma of the Nepal Prajatantrik Mahasabha, were arrested along with many of their party workers. These leaders were released almost immediately, with one or two exceptions, and they shortly thereafter issued statements lauding the King's action. Enthusiasm among the party leaders diminished perceptibly after the appointment of the new Cabinet, dominated by former Nepali Congress leaders and independents, and turned to frustration when it became apparent that the King had no intention of lifting the ban on political parties.

Subsequent events seem to indicate that some of the opposition party leaders were not nearly so enthusiastic about the December *coup* as the statements issued at the time of their release from detention would suggest. Several leaders, including Bhadrakali Mishra of the Praja Parishad and Kashi Prasad Shrivastav of the United Democratic party, fled to India in early 1961 and joined the Nepali Congress. For the most part, none of these represented a significant accretion of strength to the Nepali Congress, since they lacked anything more than local centers of support in Nepal. Nor could they even be considered as unofficial spokesmen for their former party comrades in Nepal, who almost without exception vehemently denounced them as traitors to party principles.

Quite a different matter, however, was the flight to India of Bharat Shamsher, the dominant personality in the Gorkha Parishad. Bharat Shamsher was arrested on December 15, 1960, and was not released for nearly three months, long after the other opposition party leaders had been set free. On obtaining his release from detention, the Gorkha Parishad leader issued a statement supporting the king's action, but later claimed that it had been extracted from him under duress. Like most of the other party leaders, he was restricted to Kathmandu Valley for some months. Eventually he received permission to pay short visits to India and Europe. He made two trips abroad, returning each time as scheduled. In the fall of 1961, however, he started off once again, this time not to return. The first indication that this trip differed from his previous excursions was Bharat Shamsher's unexpected attendance at the Rome session of the Second (Socialist) International. On returning to India in November, he held a press conference in New Delhi in which he denounced the royal regime in the strongest possible language and declared his intention to cooperate with the Nepali Congress in a joint effort to overthrow it. Slightly more than a month later, he announced the merger of the Gorkha Parishad with the Nepali Congress, which he described as "a cause, a conviction, and a platform for all democrats," and said that his party's action was guided by the belief that differences in details of programme have to be sacrificed for a bigger cause."

The alliance between the Nepali Congress and the Bharat Shamsher wing of the Gorkha Parishad constituted a potentially serious threat to the King, since it brought a number of trained party workers in various parts of the hill areas of Nepal within the opposition camp. Although Gorkha Parishad leaders in Kathmandu hastened to denounce their erstwhile leader, there are reasons for assuming that Bharat Shamsher, with his well-lined pocketbook, retained the loyalty of several party units outside the capital.

Within the Nepali Congress, according to reports, Bharat Shamsher has been a consistent advocate of revolutionary tactics, and several of the armed attacks on government posts in the hill areas in 1962 were allegedly undertaken by his supporters. Indeed, a decided change in character in Nepali Congress tactics seems to have followed the merger with the Gorkha Parishad. The earlier armed outbreaks in Nepal were hastily and cursorily executed and seemed to be incited for their nuisance value. By February, 1962, the raids were better planned, were carried out on a larger and more ambitious scale, and at times seemed to be genuinely revolutionary in character. Whether this reflected Bharat Shamsher's influence or a change in objective conditions in Nepal, the results were the same—a decided worsening of relations between the Nepali Congress leaders in exile and the King.

"Loyal" Former Party Leaders

Many of the political party leaders in Nepal have successfully avoided both imprisonment and exile since the December *coup* and have remained around Kathmandu awaiting the magic touch from the palace. Some, like Dilli Raman Regmi, have dropped quietly out of the public eye. Others, such as Tanka Prasad Acharya and Ranga Nath Sharma, have been consistent and vocal supporters of the King and vociferous critics of the Nepali Congress. Rather disappointingly the tangible benefits accruing to them for their forthright stand have been few and far between. Appointments to minor, usually semiofficial posts have been forthcoming for some of them, but the highly coveted ministerial appointments have gone to former Nepali Congress members and to "independents." Yet there is always the possibility that the King's favour might turn their way, and they stand ready and eager to serve when the call is heard. In a somewhat special category is K. I. Singh, who has kept carefully out of politics but has threatened on a number of occasions to lead a mass movement against the present regime if the political atmosphere did not improve.

All of the anti-Nepali Congress political leaders have chafed under the regulations banning party activity and have sought to circumvent these restrictions in various ways, with Tanka Prasad Acharya usually taking the lead in these maneuvers. The former Prime Minister first attempted to obtain the King's approval for the formation of a "country-wide nonpolitical organization on a democratic basis" to assist the government in the struggle against "antinational elements both inside and outside the country." Six leaders from the Praja Parishad, Nepal Prajatantrik Mahasabha, and the United Democratic party (though K. I. Singh kept strictly away from these maneuvers) submitted to the King a petition which stressed the usefulness of such an organization for inculcating nationalist sentiment among the people and resisting "antinational" elements. Also the organization would, it was claimed, "resist and expose the design of any foreign country which might attempt to exercise pressure on Nepali, bring before the government and the people any defects in the policy and work of the Nepal Government," and cooperate in "democratic and constructive tasks."

In replying to the petition, the government expressed its appreciation of the patriotism of the political leaders who had come to realize the need to resist "antinational" forces, and said that it was "always prepared to encourage and extend cooperation to any organized popular force honestly resisting traitorous activities." The reply went on to say, however: "...a ban has been imposed on political organizations at present, [and] the government is unable to permit any organization to assume a political colour." Tanka Prasad and the other politicians were uncertain as to whether this reply was to be interpreted as a rejection or an approval of their request to form a "nonpolitical" organization and a clarification was sought. The government's reply to this second communication was unequivocal. The objectives mentioned in the petition, the

Secretary of the National Guidance Ministry stated, demonstrated beyond doubt that the proposed organization would be "political in character." The political leaders were then reminded of the Home Ministry's notification of December 10, 1961, banning all organized political activity. It was the decision of His Majesty's Government that no permission could be granted to form such an organization.

Thwarted in this endeavour, Tanka Prasad moved to achieve his objective through other tactics. At the Intellectual's Conference held in Kathmandu in June, 1962, the Praja Parishad leader launched a bitter attack on the Council of Ministers and the policy under which "innocent political parties" which supported the King and were "prepared to work for the interest of the country" were penalized for the "misdeeds of a particular party." He suggested that these parties should be allowed to function, while the ban should be retained on "offending" parties such as the Nepali Congress. He waxed particularly indignant over what he alleged was the tendency of some of the present Ministers to argue that if the King should have to replace them, the only "deserving" alternative was the Nepali Congress.

Tanka Prasad has also been the only political leader of note to respond favourably, even enthusiastically, to the Communist party's proposal for a united front, which he apparently views as a vehicle for his reentry into active politics. But the government has not responded any more favourably to this proposal than it did to Tanka Prasad's earlier bid to form a "non-political" national organization. Frustration continues to be the lot of most of the leaders of the minor political parties, who see little future for themselves in the present administrative structure and even fewer opportunities in any political system in which the Nepali Congress would play an important role. Their only chance for proper recognition seems to be in the hope that developments inside and outside Nepal might force the King to turn to them for support and cooperation.

Nonparty Political Elites

Since December, 1960, King Mahendra has moved, and with some success, to provide as broad a base for his regime as circumstances permitted. One aspect of the current situation that distinguishes the present system from earlier direct-rule periods is the great emphasis the King has placed upon youth in the governmental reorganization. Three of the dominating personalities in the first post-*coup* Cabinet were in their thirties and a number of other men as young or younger were given high posts in the Secretariat. In most instances these were well-educated young Nepalese who had pursued advanced studies in Western or Indian universities and whose ideas and ideals contrasted in many ways with those held by the older, tradition-oriented groups upon whom the King had depended in the past. This emphasis upon youth serves a dual purpose for the King. In the first place, it provides him with a base, and a comparatively competent one technically, upon which he can depend for support in pressing economic and other reforms. At the same time, it associates with the royal regime some of the potential leaders of Nepali society and satisfies their ambitions, at least temporarily, by giving them a status they would not normally attain for another decade.

Presumably King Mahendra hoped and expected that this policy would gain for him wide support among members of the young educated class in Nepal, who would appreciate the new opportunities for advancement opened to them. The response from the young intellectuals has not been altogether positive, as many in this group seem to feel that their view of the world and that of the place are incompatible. This is not to imply that there is a revolutionary spirit among the young intellectuals, even potentially. On the contrary, cynicism rather than radicalism seems to be the prevailing mood, and there is little to indicate that they are prepared to serve as the core of an opposition movement to the regime, even though few of them may be ideologically in step with the King's political programme. The future trends, however, as much less clear and will probably depend upon how this group fares under the present system. Of some significance in this respect is the rapid increase in educated unemployment, previously a minor problem. Many talented young Nepalese are now obtaining higher education, either in Nepal or abroad, without any concomitant expansion of employment opportunities.

While making an appeal to the young educated Nepalese, the King has not neglected the groups which have traditionally held a dominant position in the various institutions of government and which have generally supported the crown *vis-a-vis* the political parties. In contrast to the policy initiated by the Nepali Congress government, in which such considerations received little attention, the King has reinstituted in its essentials the old system under which certain categories of posts were the virtual preserve of caste or ethnic groups. Most of the King's appointments to the judiciary, for instance, have been Brahmans, the caste that has traditionally filled such posts. Economic vested-interest groups were also guaranteed an important voice in such bodies as the Royal Land Reform Commission and the Royal Taxation Commission, set up to advise the government on economic policies in these crucial spheres. The National Planning Council, which was given the delicate task of preparing a detailed development plan for the country, represented an intricate balancing of economic and political groups having a vested interest in these proceedings if not, unfortunately, much expertise in the task of planning. The far-ranging reforms projected for the land tenure and revenue systems have also been carefully devised not to infringe upon the ancient privileges enjoyed by the landowning classes of the important Kirati and Limbu communities of eastern Nepal. All things considered, the King has been remarkably successful in retaining the support of these normally conservative groups even while advocating economic and political reforms which may prove potentially detrimental to their interests.

The King's handling of the political parties has been no less skillful, if not always so successful. Since his ascent to the throne in 1955, King Mahendra has developed several techniques designed to frustrate the functioning of the political party system. One that was employed with considerable success on at least two occasions before 1959 involved the holding of all-inclusive conferences to which the King invited representatives of innumerable (and sometimes fictitious) political, social, regional, and ethnic organizations. Called theoretically to ascertain public opinion on national issues, the conferences were also used to exacerbate differences between the various political party factions; at the same time they served as platforms for the expression of antiparty views by otherwise anonymous nonpolitical personalities. Their ultimate effect in the past had been to sabotage efforts currently under way to rationalize the party system through a process of amalgamation into three or four basic groups. The way in which minor local parties and "parallel" parties were granted equal status at the conference with the few broader-based parties served to encourage the former to maintain their separate existence. The inclusion of nonpolitical organizations in the conferences was also a useful device for dramatizing one of the King's main criticisms of the party system, namely, that the parties represented special and personal interests rather than the national interest.

The Intellectual's Conference at Kathmandu in June, 1962, exhibited a slight variation on this technique. The ban on political parties obviated the necessity of aiming the conference directly at the subversion of the party system, but it did serve to emphasize the differences in the approaches of the various political party leaders and to obstruct any tendency toward the formation of working agreements among them. It also provided the party leaders—or, rather, those acceptable to the regime—with an opportunity to vent their criticisms of the administration in public without in any way obligating the government to heed their views. The Conference thus served as a substitute of sorts for a Parliament and at the same time suffered from none of the defects, from the King's point of view, of a parliamentary system.

But probably the greatest advantage the King has enjoyed in his relations with the political party movement is the community of interest on certain basic questions between the palace and most of the political party leadership outside of the Nepali Congress. Even after the introduction of parliamentary democracy, the opposition parties displayed a marked preference for traditional political tactics—intrigue, conspiracy, and Court politics. The one unforgivable transgression of the Nepali Congress in the eyes of both the palace and the opposition parties was its refusal to confine itself to these traditional tactics and its increasing emphasis upon alternative approaches to political office and power. The threat was all the more real because the Nepali Congress won an overwhelming victory in the 1959 elections and seemed then to be on the verge of establishing a monolithic party system which would have relegated both the palace and the opposition parties to a permanent position of inferiority.

The opposition parties, therefore, deemed a political system dominated by the Nepali Congress to be more detrimental to their interests than one in which the palace was the source of authority and the dispenser of political rewards. It was with their general approbation that King Mahendra reintroduced the traditional political pattern after the December *coup* and retained it subsequently as an essential characteristic of his new political system. These are the politics with which most party leaders are familiar and within which they can function comfortably and with some degree of sophistication. It is, indeed, paradoxical that political parties, which in view of their public stances and proclaimed ideologies should have been political innovators and apostles of modernization, have served as powerful supports to the traditional political pattern. In the process, moreover, the parties have also been instrumental in solidifying the preeminent position of the monarchy through their readiness to accept the palace as the source of ultimate political authority. In the final analysis, however, it has been the King who has been enabled to use the party leaders for his own purposes, rather than the reverse.

4

The Royal Regime and Its Policies

To the Surprise of most observers, the radical political changes introduced in Nepal since December 15, 1960, have not been accompanied by substantive changes in policies and programmes in most other spheres. Trends in economic, social, administrative, and foreign policy that had been evident at least since 1955, and, in some instances, even in the latter stages of the Rana period, have continued. The royal regime has not represented a significant break with the past and, indeed, the differences that can be perceived are essentially those involving modes of operations and tactics rather than basic objectives.

There was initially considerable confusion about objectives after the *coup*, as some of King Mahendra's earliest pronouncements seemed to imply that major changes in the government's economic, administrative, and foreign policy were imminent. The tone of the Royal Proclamation of December 15 on land reform, taxation, and administrative reorganization, for instance, was such as to encourage the assumption that the new regime would abandon or seriously modify these programmes. In retrospect, however, these statements would seem to have been contrived carefully to elicit the maximum political support from those political and economic vested-interest groups that had been hostile to the Nepali Congress without in fact obligating the new government to any definite action.

Land Reform

Land legislation enacted between 1951 and 1960 had been restricted to reform of the tenure system, rent control, and protection of tenancy rights. Policy on these issues had been defined most comprehensively in the 1957 Lands Act and the 1959 Birta Abolition Act, although neither programme had been implemented with conspicuous vigour or with any notable improvement in the status and position of tenants. Even the Nepali Congress government had moved cautiously on land reform, despite its self-proclaimed adherance to a democratic-socialist ideology.

In the Royal Proclamation of January 5, 1961, King Mahendra stated that the government would "profit by past experience [and] achieve this objective [*Birta* abolition] by means of a clear and scientific policy." This had been generally construed to mean that the 1959 Birta Abolition Act would be implemented in a milder form, if at all. The appointment of a Royal Commission on Taxation and Birta Abolition on February 6, "to submit recommendations with regard to *Birta* abolition" reinforced this impression. Holders of *Birta* land were particularly encouraged by the broad representation they obtained on the Commission, which assured them an important voice in its proceedings. As expected, the Commission's report, submitted to the government on March 27, suggested major revisions in the programme, recommending that it be restricted to the imposition of taxes on *Birta* lands at 50 per cent of the rate on adjoining non-*Birta* lands and that the system itself should not be abolished except for *Birta* lands acquired by Ranas after 1847. This report naturally aroused expectations that the abolition programme would be drastically amended, and it was an unpleasant shock to *Birta* holders when Finance Minister Rishikesh Shah announced in his budget speech in August that the programme would be implemented with only slight modifications. That the report had made little impact on the government was further demonstrated in the Amendment of the 1959 Birta Abolition Act, promulgated on February 6, 1962, which virtually ignored the Commission's recommendations.

In line with its announced intention to reappraise land legislation, the royal regime appointed a second advisory body, the Royal Commission on Land Reform, in June, 1961, headed by Tanka Prasad Acharya, but including conservative landowning interests. The report it eventually submitted seems to have been no more successful in influencing government policy than that of its predecessor. In any case, the Agricultural (New Arrangements) Act promulgated on April 12, 1963, not only retained intact most of the controversial provisions of the 1957 Lands Act, but also introduced a radical innovation in land policy by imposing ceilings on the size of landholdings. Surplus lands acquired by the government under this programme were to be redistributed with tenants and landless labour having first priority on their purchase.

The procedures adopted in implementing the land redistribution programme, however, seemed to guarantee that the immediate impact would be negligible. The government decided, and announced at the time of the Act's promulgation, that this measure would initially be implemented only on an experimental basis in a few villages in three districts. Nor were the requisite supplementary ordinances enacted to bar the transfer of ownership of land within the family or to traditional familial retainers. In private, the government frankly admitted that the programme was unlikely to result in the redistribution of much land, except possibly in a few areas in the Terai.

The Act was defended on the grounds that it would lead to the breakup of large landholdings by forcing redistribution *within* landowning families. This sophisticated, if somewhat obtuse argument presumed that such rdistribution would serve the dual purpose of encouraging the disintegration of the joint family system and improving agricultural production methods. Smaller holdings, it was argued, would force landowners to cultivate the land themselves and utilize improved methods of production. Obviously, this would do little to improve the condition of tenants and landless labourers.

The "redistribution" principle in the 1963 Act, thus, may have had more of the character of a radical slogan than of a fundamental land-reform programme, but the long-term effects of the acceptance of land redistribution as official policy should not be underestimated. Nor should it be assumed that the timidity displayed by the government in the early stages of implementing this programme necessarily implies that it will not be applied with more determination in the future. In 1964 a slightly more stringent version of the 1963 Act was promulgated to plug a few of the many loopholes of the earlier legislation. The most important and controversial innovation was the clause which set ceilings on landholdings by family (defined to include parents, minor sons, and unmarried daughters) rather than individuals, thus complicating the subdivision of holdings within a family. The government has also shortened the target period during which the land-reform programme is to be implemented throughout Nepal to three years (*i.e.*, 1964-67).

Trade and Commerce

Fundamental dissatisfaction with the system under which Nepal traded abroad has been a constant feature of Nepali politics since 1951. Because more than 95 per cent of Nepal's trade is with India, Indo-Nepali relations have been vitally affected by the gradual crystallization of opinion. The terms of trade with and through India, as prescribed in the 1950 trade treaty, have received the most concentrated criticism, but there has also been widespread resentment at the virtually total dependence upon India for Nepal's general economic well-being. To the educated elite, Nepal's independence and national sovereignty will never be complete without extensive modifications in the trade structure and a reduction of Nepal's exposure to Indian economic domination.

The uncompromisingly aggressive nationalistic posture of the royal regime has placed it directly within the mainstream of articulate Nepali opinion on this subject. Shortly after assuming control in December, 1960, the new government announced its intention to continue the efforts undertaken by previous regimes to diversify Nepal's trade structure. The steady deterioration in Indo-Nepali relations throughout 1961 and 1962 enhanced the importance of this programme as Kathmandu grew increasingly concerned with the possibility that Indian economic pressure might be employed to force political changes in Nepal. Presumably it was to counter this potentiality that King Mahendra first approached China and Pakistan in 1961 in search of alternative channels for Nepal's trade and commerce. While the terms of these proposals were markedly different from those advanced by previous governments, they represented the logical extension of Nepal's efforts since 1947 to expand political and economic relations with countries other than India.

The agreement signed with Communist China in October, 1961, while King Mahendra was on a state visit to that country, provided for a potentially significant contribution to greater flexibility in Nepal's trading system. Pakistan agreed to finance and supervise the construction of a road connecting Kathmandu with Kodari, a village on the Nepal-Tibet border. It is widely assumed in Nepal that this road, by facilitating trade with Tibet and China, will open another market for Nepal's products and a new source for manufactured goods. Even more important is the expectation that Kathmandu will reemerge as the principle entrepot for trade between India and Tibet, a status that contributed to Nepal's affluence for several centuries before the opening of the shorter and easier route through Sikkim around the turn of the century, lately closed by the Sino-Indian border dispute. The regulate the terms of trade between Nepal and Tibet, a new trade agreement was signed by Kathmandu and Peking on May 19, 1964. This agreement, however, was not nearly so comprehensive as had been predicted in certain quarters in Nepal, for it ignored many of the complaints about the treatment of Nepali traders in Tibet that has hampered commercial relations in recent years.

Another aspect of China's economic aid programme in Nepal that has affected established trade patterns is the system under which China has provided consumers' goods free of cost to the Nepal government, the goods later being sold on the local market. The funds thus acquired are used to meet Nepali currency requirements for local Chinese aid projects. Because these goods are priced artificially to compete with similar goods imported from or through India, they find a ready market in Kathmandu. Presumably this practice will continue only so long as Chinese aid projects require local currency and less clumsy and expensive means for its acquisition are not available. But in the prosess China has gained some tangential political benefits and, at the same time, has won a foothold in the Kathmandu market for Chinese-produced commodities that on strictly economic terms of trade could not compete with Indian imports.

Pakistan probably plays an even more important part in Nepal's trade diversification plans than China. In Septemper, 1961, King Mahendra paid a state visit to West Pakistan, in the course of which he suggested expanded commercial relations between the two countries. In response a Pakistani trade delegation came to Kathmandu in April, 1962, for preliminary talks on a trade agreement. A Nepali delegation returned the visit a few months later, and on October 19 a trade treaty was signed, providing mutual most-favoured-nation treatment. A series of talks in Karachi in January, 1963, culminated in the signing of a trade and transit treaty providing for the free movement of goods between the two countries without custom or transit duties. Air service inaugurated between East Pakistan and Kathmandu in 1963, gave Nepali importers an alternative to Calcutta as a transit port for goods purchased abroad.

In conjunction with these efforts to diversify Nepal's traditional trade pattern, the royal regime has also sought to improve the terms of trade with India or in transit through India. From the economic point of view, the successes achieved here have been of the utmost significance, since the preponderance of Nepal's trade is still with India and is steadily expanding.

An Indo-Nepali agreement signed on May 14, 1961, relaxed certain of the procedures under which imports and passenger baggage were transported through India. Irksome features of the 1950 trade treaty system were further reduced by the abolition of the bonding system for Nepali imports in transit through India in October, 1963, and the simplification of the central excise duty refund procedures in January, 1964.

These concessions from New Delhi have gone a long way toward satisfying Nepal's basic objective—recognition of the right of unrestricted transit of goods through India. In furthering its campaign on this question, Kathmandu has actively aligned itself with other landlocked countries at a number of international conferences in pressing for the recognition of the "right of free transit" as an integral part of international law.

The progress made toward trade diversification has had important political implications in Nepal, where it is interpreted as symbolizing fuller recognition of the country's sovereign status, but the immediate economic impact has been slight. Trade with Pakistan and China in 1963 was less than 3 per cent of the total recorded transactions and still less if the widespread and largely unrecorded local trade in agricultural products between the Nepal Terai and the adjoining Indian districts is taken into consideration. The volume of trade with Pakistan and China is likely to grow substantially in absolute terms in the next decade, but its proportion in Nepal's total trade structure may not increase proportionately, as trade with India is also growing rapidly. Moreover, some of the political considerations that made it incumbent upon Nepal to seek alternative trade channels in 1961 and 1962 are no longer as persuasive, while most of the features of the trade system with India that were found objectionable have now been abolished or modified. Diversification is still a stated objective of Nepal's trade policy, but probably is not assigned so high a priority as it was in 1961. There has been an increasing recognition in Kathmandu that Nepal's "natural" trade lines are with India, and somewhat less reluctance to accept certain economic consequences inherent in this situation.

Industrial Policy

In Nepal, as in most "developing" nations, there is a tendency to view industrialization as the remedy for all of the country's economic ills. But industrial expansion since 1951 has been insignificant and directly attributable to foreign aid or Indian investment. A comprehensive industrial policy was not even evolved until the Nepali Congress took office in 1959. The royal regime has retained the essential features of this industrial policy, liberalizing even further the conditions under which both local and foreign capital can invest in industry. The 1950 Company Act was amended in 1961 and an Industrial Enterprises Act was promulgated in 1962. Under the provisions of these laws, new industries, whether foreign or indigenous, have been granted a ten-year exemption from income tax and are permitted to spend up to 70 per cent of their hard-currency earnings on the import of machinery and spare parts. Foreign investors are allowed to repatriate as profits 10 per cent of their capital investment in hard currency annually. A government-sponsored organization, Sajha, has been established to extend financial and other assistance to co-operative industrial and commercial ventures.

Official projections of industrial expansion in Nepal place little stress on private domestic investment. Most new industries scheduled for completion within the next few years are dependent upon foreign aid, either public or private. Several small factories are being constructed under the Russian and Chinese aid programmes. The Indian and American aid programmes have so far adjurned direct involvement in the construction of factories, but have each financed industrial estates near Kathmandu in which a number of private small-scale industries are located. The gevernment has also been negotiating with several Indian industrial firms and with a number of European and Asian governments and private firms in its search for sources of capital investment in industry.

Foreign aid in industrialization has led to some curious misconceptions in Nepal. It is frequently asserted, for instance, that China and Russia support Nepal's industrialization, because they are building a few small factories, while the United States and India are secretly opposed to it—reputedly for capitalist-imperialist motives. What is usually ignored in these allegations is the role played by the United States and India in the development of communications and the expansion of power resources, obvious prerequisites for any serious industrialization programme. Indeed, even the Russian and Chinese factories would have been imposible without the roads and power provided by American and Indian aid projects.

The Role of Foreign Aid

Among Asian states there is perhaps none whose economic development programme is so dependent upon foreign assistance as is that of Nepal. In the 1963/64 budget estimates, for instance, more than 70 per cent of Nepali development expenditure allocations represented foreign assistance. Even these figures were probably misleading, for the estimated revenue resources of the government covered less than 40 per cent of its share of the development budget. When the various other types of indirect assistance are also taken into consideration, it is probable that the proportion of foreign aid in Nepal's development programme is close to 85 or 20 per cent. And even then, only around 50 per cent of the funds allocated for development purposes has usually been expended in any single year.

This situation has never been a very happy one from the Nepali viewpoint. The Nepali Congress government, on assuming office in 1959, spoke of the necessity of reducing dependence on foreign aid; but by the time the 1960/61 budget was introduced there was a frank admittance that this goal was unrealistic and would be for some time. Nepal's problem, it was admitted, was to attract more foreign aid and to rationalize the system under which this aid was utilized.

A similar pattern has been evident under the royal regime. In his first budget speech (1961/62), Finance Minister

Rishikesh Shah emphasized the need to increase Nepal's proportionate contribution to the development budget; but by the time of his second budget speech (1962/63), this objective received scant attention. The 1963/64 budget speech by the new Finance Minister, Surya Bahadur Thapa, raised the subject once again, but in such terms as to make it apparent that any major reduction in the foreign aid proportion of the development budget was unlikely because of the lack of substantial new sources of indigenous revenue.

The reliance upon foreign aid, unavoidable though it may be in the circumstances, complicates the government's task in formulating a well conceived and comprehensive programme of economic development. The source of aid is undependable and is susceptible to wide fluctuations—at times, for reasons having nothing to do with Nepal. The cement factory promised by Peking in 1956 and again in 1960, for instance, was suddenly canceled in 1964 after surveys conducted by Chinese technicians had approved the project site. The official explanation given was the unsuitability of the site selected, presumably because of the unavailability of adequate supplies of raw materials. But according to other reports, China had to back down at the last moment because the equipment for the factory, which was to have been purchased in Czechoslavakia, was no longer available, owing to the deterioration in Sino-Soviet relations. It can be presumed that these reports are reliable, for Peking did not merely ask to shift the site of the factory, but dropped the project altogether, placing the Nepal government in an awkward situation. Cement is badly required for Nepal's housing and development programmes. In 1964, therefore, Kathmandu had to start searching for alternative sources of foreign aid for the construction of a cement factory, at least five years later than would have been the case if reliance had not been placed upon the Chinese commitment.

Under such circumstances, it is difficult for Nepal to evolve a coordinated programme of economic development. The four primary sources of foreign aid—the United States, India, the Soviet Union, and China—have different motivations in offering aid and radically different approaches. The Russians and Chinese prefer short-term projects that will make an immediate impact upon the Nepali public, while the United States and India have concentrated upon more basic, long-term programmes in such areas as education, agriculture, communications, and power. Nepali views on priorities in economic development have to be fitted into this complex structure, and it is little wonder that the government has never really attempted to conceptualize a pattern of economic development that is anything more than a collection of unrelated and sometimes inconsistent development projects. The Nepal government is in no position to extend much practical guidance to the foreign aid agencies in formulating their programmes, much less to insist that they conform to an established pattern. As a result, the foreign sources of aid often decide what is to be offered, and the Nepal government has no alternative but to accept, even when the programmes do not conform to its own priority schedule.

This situation is in part a consequence of the Nepal government's decision to seek the maximum diversification of sources of foreign aid, as it does in trade and commerce. Too great a reliance on a single source of aid is considered prejudicial to Nepal's independence and nonalignment policy since there is the assumption—doubtless, correct—that all foreign economic aid programmes have a political motivation. Nepali nationalism, which is intensely sensitive to any threat of manipulation from without, prefers a disorganized approach to economic development in which coordination between the various aid programmes is kept to a minimum. Indeed, the most telling charges levied against the American programme in Nepal is that it works too closely with the Indian programme in formulating and proposing development projects. This indicates plainly that in Nepal, as in most other "newly emerging" nations, political considerations have precedence over economic progress.

Social Reform

One of the most widely publicized programmes of the royal regime is the new Legal Code promulgated in April, 1963. Certain sections of the old Muluki Ain were radically amended to remove provisions based on essentially nonegalitarian, traditional Hindu social concepts. Discrimination on the basis of caste was forbidden, intercaste marriages were legalized, polygamy was prohibited, and women were guaranteed certain rights with regard to divorce and inheritance previously denied them. August 17, 1963, the date of the enforcement of the new Legal Code, was celebrated in Kathmandu, with untouchables assuming a prominent role in the festivities.

Subsequently, however, the government has moved with caution in interpreting and implementing some of the new legal provisions. In a clarification issued four months later by the Special Complaints Department of the Palace Secretariat it was announced that the caste system itself had not been abolished. The new code, it was explained, "seeks only to introduce equality before the law." The position was made quite clear in the next sentence: "Those who indulge in actions prejudicial to the social customs and traditions of others will be punished." Attempts by untouchables to force an entry into Pashupatinath, the holiest of Hindu temples in Nepal, were forestalled by the police, reportedly on the grounds that the social customs and traditions of high caste Hindus were infringed upon by these actions.

King Mahendra himself issued a cautionary warning in March, 1964, when he stated at a civic reception in western Nepal that "social-reform cannot be achieved all of a sudden... least of all by strict legislation." He explained that the new code had been devised so that people could easily observe its provisions, and that society was not to be disrupted in the name of reform. That same month, a five-member Law Commission to study defects in the new Legal Code, "which was hastily drafted by the former Law Commission," was appointed by the government.

Despite the government's apparent responsiveness to the objections raised by some traditionalist elements, the social reforms introduced are likely to be retained. It is an interesting commentary on Nepali politics that the present regime, which draws its most important support from conservative groups with a vested interest in the *status quo*, was able to introduce a social reform programme more radical than anything projected by the democratic-socialist Nepali Congress. Here, again, the need for the regime to assume a progressive facade that appeals to younger educated groups, but to implement its programme in such a way as not to alienate conservative supporters, is in evidence.

Administrative Reorganization

Every major political upheaval in Nepal since 1951 had been accompanied by substantial changes in top administrative positions, and the December, 1960, *coup* was no exception. Indeed, the most thorough overhaul of the Secretariat yet attempted in postrevolutionary Nepal occurred in the first year after the *coup*. Civil servants suspected of too close ties to the Nepali Congress were dismissed at all levels of administration and in all branches of government, including the judiciary. The exact number dismissed is difficult to determine from published sources, as district and local level dismissals were never summarized or even reported. The Nepali Congress has placed the number at five thousand, which may be somewhat exaggerated; but if dismissals at all levels of government service are included, it is probable that three thousand is a reliable figure. New appointments to higher administrative posts were openly based upon political considerations, and merit or qualifications were, at best, incidental factors. The Public Service Commission was ignored, its powers being suspended in whole or in part during most of this crucial transitional period.

The procedures adopted by the royal regime in this wholesale purge of administrative personnel nullified and even reversed the efforts made since 1954 to provide some degree of tenure security through the basing of appointments and promotions on merit and seniority. Once the purge was completed, however, the royal regime effected a partial return to the trend toward the standardization of civil service procedures, giving added emphasis to nonpolitical criteria for all but the higher category of posts. But the psychological impact of the massive administrative reorganization in 1961 is still evident. On three occasions since 1955 King Mahendra has suspended established administrative procedures to initiate large-scale changes in personnel, and there is no assurance that this will not occur again. Government servants have been criticized by the press and political groups for allegedly being more concerned with strengthening their contacts with the palace or Ministry than in the competent performance of their duties. But is it reasonable to expect anything else when security of tenure is based upon arbitrary rather than formalized procedures?

The royal regime has not restricted itself to changes in personnel. It has projected reforms in the administrative structure. Probably the most significant, potentially, is the proposed decentralization of the administration to parallel the decentralized political system under Panchayat Raj. In 1962, a new regional structure was superimposed upon the old district administrative system, dividing Nepal into fourteen zones and seventy-five Development Districts which coincide with the territorial jurisdiction of the zonal and district panchayats.

The pattern of administrative decentralization is still unclear in several important respects, and some of the basic policies announced earlier are under periodic reconsideration. A Deconcentration Committee, headed by Vishwabandhu Thapa, was appointed in 1963, but its report merely approved the general policy of decentralization and made little positive contribution to the resolution of the problems this policy has raised.

Doubtless, the most crucial question facing the government at present is the conflict in jurisdiction which has arisen between the various regional units of administration and led to serious confusion as to their respective spheres of authority. The government announced that the old administrative districts were to be abolished eventually, and that the administrative functions of the Bada Hakims would be transferred to the district panchayats. But when this finally occurred in 1965, the Bada Hakim's powers and functions were transferred to centrally appointed zonal commissioners rather than district panchayats.

Confusion is further compounded by the existence of Zonal Commissioners and Zonal Guidance Officers, appointed by the Central Secretariat, and zonal panchayats elected by the district panchayats, all with vaguely defined and often conflicting spheres of authority within the same territorial jurisdiction as the district panchayats and Bada Hakims. Furthermore, several Ministries and Departments of the central government have their own personnel in the field, and the lines of authority for these officials have not been clearly defined as yet. A Conference of Zonal Commissioners was held in Kathmandu in May, 1964, to study this situation, but no substantive recommendations were forthcoming, except for the usual warning that the government must move cautiously in implementing the decentralization policy.

And there is no doubt that this is the approach adopted by the government, which has moved slowly on the more complex aspects of decentralization and fairly rapidly only when the changes involved a minimal disruption of the existing administrative process. Nor is there any doubt that the Central Secratariat retains final discretionary authority in all administrative matters. The lower tiers of the panchayat system would seem to have been created for two purposes: to fill a serious lacuna in the old administrative system that limited the efficacy of the Central Secretariat's authority in the less accessible areas of the country, and to assist the programme of economic development. The decentralization of administrative power so far projected concerns primarily activities essential to the successful exercise of these functions. As such, they involve more the decentralization of duties than of decision-making powers, which are still retained by the Central Secretariat on most important subjects. Thus, the policy of the royal regime on the role of panchayats does not differ markedly from that adopted by previous governments which also projected a limited devolution of functions to local and regional political and administrative units.

International Relations

In dismissing the Nepali Congress government, King Mahendra implied that disagreements over foreign policy had been a major factor in his decision. B.P. Koirala and his colleagues were accused of planning to merge Nepal with a neighbouring country—never specified, but presumably India—and with having encouraged "antinational" elements, again presumably pro-India groups in Nepal. But there was little in the King's subsequent actions to indicate that there had really been any serious disagreement over the basic principles of Nepal's foreign policy, including such controversial issues as the Gandak treaty and other agreements with India, all of which have been retained.

The differences between the royal regime and the Nepali Congress on foreign policy would seem to have been primarily over the interpretation of certain of these basic principles and, even more important, over the tactics used to achieve policy objectives. "Equal friendship with India and China" was the policy of both but the term apparently had different meanings for King Mahendra and B.P. Koirala. For political considerations that were essentially domestic, the royal regime permitted and up to October, 1962, even seemed to encourage developments that were likely to disrupt relations with India. The Nepali press, fairly strictly controlled in most other respects, was allowed to indulge in bitter anti-Indian campaigns, often drawing upon the reported remarks of Ministers for support and verification. A similar license was not extended to the anti-Communist or anti-Chinese journals, which occasionally had to suspend publication temporarily because of remarks about Nepal's northern neighbour that were no more critical than those permitted about its southern neighbour.

The royal regime also published even more vigorously the policy of expanding Nepal's international relations, with particular emphasis placed upon association with African and Asian powers that followed a policy of nonalignment. Nepal's position on nonalignment and East-West "cold war" issues coincides closely to that followed by India, the objective being maximum contacts with both sides and the avoidance of any direct formal obligations to either. But nonalignment also has a special connotation for Nepal in view of the country's strategic location in an area in which the Sino-Indian border dispute is the most pervasive fact of life. "Nonalignment" plus "equal friendship" equals "neutrality" as far as Nepal is concerned, even though this is neutrality in a dispute between a member of the nonaligned bloc of nations and a Communist state.

Kathmandu has tried to extract recognition of its neutral status from both of its giant neighbours. But there are serious complications in implementing a neutralist policy which is contradictory to some aspects of Nepal's international obligations and internal policy. Nepal cannot simply ignore, for instance, the 1950 treaty of peace and friendship with India which places Nepal in an unofficial alliance with India, the sizable "Gurkha" recruitment for the Indian military forces, the Indian military posts at most key pass areas on the Nepal-Tibet border, and the important role played by Indian military advisers in the reorganization and rearmament of the Nepal state army. When these tangible factors are combined with the intimate social, cultural, economic, and historical ties that have existed between India and Nepal for at least milleniums, and the incompatibility of Chinese communism and Nepal's social structure and polity, neutrality is possible only as long as the Sino-Indian dispute does not explode into full-scale war.

The delicacy of Nepal's position in the Himalayan border area was dramatically revealed in October, 1962, when Chinese forces launched limited attacks on the extremities of the Sino-Indian frontier—Ladakh and North East Frontier Agency. Kathmandu's response to this critical situation, which at times threatened to expand into a larger conflict, presumably was indicative of its fundamental position in inter-Himalayan politics. Alarmed by the inexpected upsetting of the balance of power in the border area, so vital to Nepal's continuation as an independent entity, Kathmandu moved quickly to improve relations with India. As an earnest of the change in attitude, there was a virtually total cessation of the bitter charges and countercharges that had been exchanged almost daily between the two governments. Kathmandu also refused to heed the suggestion, reportedly from Peking, that "Gurkhas" in Indian military service be recalled or at least barred from service on the disputed border as a token of Nepal's neutrality in the dispute.

Indo-Nepali relations were placed upon a new basis in 1963 by the visit of several Indian leaders, including Home Minister Lal Bahadur Shastri, the Chief of Staff of the Indian Army, and President Radhakrishnan to Kathmandu and several visits by King Mahendra and his Ministers to New Delhi. In the course of the talks held on these occasions, a *rapprochement* was achieved that settled most of the political and economic issues that had previously disrupted relations between the two states. There are still several important issues upon which agreement has not been possible because the interests of the two countries, as perceived by each, diverge; but these are now kept carefully in the background by both governments in contrast to the situation up to October, 1962, when they were often exploited and emphasized.

Kathmandu has been careful to guarantee, however, that the reconciliation with India was not achieved at the expense of friendly ties with Peking. There is, perhaps, a somewhat more cautious attitude toward China, but no evident diminution in either the scope or character of their relationship. China occupies too powerful a position in the Himalayas for Nepal to risk a deterioration in relations, particularly since the defeats inflicted upon India in the 1962 border clashes with China has undermined confidence in its ability to defend Nepal's exposed and probably indefensible northern border.

Napal's relations with both the Soviet Union and the United States have assumed added importance in view of the critical situation in which it has been placed by the Sino-Indian dispute. That Kathmandu is now attempting to use these two powers as counterbalances to China, as once they were used as counter-balances to India, would seem to be suggested by the role assumed by the Soviet Union in Nepal's economic development and the officially confirmed reports that Nepal had approached the United States and the United Kingdom for military assistance. Nepal's abandonment of an isolationist policy in 1947 has brought many tangible benefits as well as psychological satisfaction for Nepali nationalist sentiment, but it has also exposed the country to numerous and conflicting pressures which threaten its very existence. The skill and tenacity with which succeeding Nepali governments have maneuvered under difficult international conditions deserves commendation. Nevertheless, it is still uncertain as to whether the short-term advantages attained will prove to have equally beneficial long-term results.

Conclusions

Viewed broadly and with a disregard of meaningless political sloganism, there has been a rather remarkable continuity in the policies and programmes adopted by the various Nepali governments since 1951. The present regime has continued for the most part the general trends established earlier, adopting a programme of cautious change directed toward the gradual modernization of the Nepali economy, social structure, and administrative system. In spite of his dependence upon the political support of conservative or reactionary elements. King Mahendra has not established an ultraconservative regime dedicated to the preservation of the *status quo.* As may be inevitable in such circumstances, however, there have been certain inconsistencies between policies as adopted and as implemented.

But the contradiction between modernization on the administrative and economic level and certain antimodernist aspects of the new political structuremay eventually power to have more serious consequences. Institutional innovations under Panchayat Raj have resulted in some changes in the channels for political activity, but have made relatively little impact upon the political process, which is still essentially traditional in character. The deficiencies of the political party system in Nepal have received ample consideration in this study. These were, nevertheless, the institutions through which the political process was being modernized—gradually and ineptly, perhaps, but with some success. The prohibition of political party activity has, thus, hampered the modernization process. King Mahendra seems to be aware of this in designing a programme to transform Nepal into a twentieth-century society, but the institutions created to replace the political parties—the lower-level panchayats and the class organizations—are of doubtful utility in carrying out this task.

This raises a critical question: Is is possible to modernize the economic, social, and administrative structures without a concomitant modernization of the political process and modes of political behaviour? This is not meant to imply that a parliamentary, democratic, or Communist system is a prerequisite to modernization; Japan proved the contrary in the nineteenth century. What would seem to be involved is the utilization of new sources of political initiative, new techniques of political organization, and new patterns in decision making, at both the administrative and the political level. It is still to be seen whether panchayats and related institutions have a positive contribution to make in this respect or whether they will obstruct, delay, and confuse the modernization process upon which Nepal's continued existence as an independent political entity may well depend.

ELECTION BRINGS STABILITY

—With the appointment of B.P. Koirala as Prime Minister of Nepal's first ever elected government the country came of age. Its experiment with democracy started in earnest. There was a constitution which guaranteed a bicameral legislature, an independent judiciary and certain justiciable fundamental rights which promised a relatively rational polity. The Nepalese Parliament was not sovereign in the sense this word is generally understood in a democratic society. For the Constitution allowed every lever of power to remain in the safe-keeping of the Palace. Despite this, Prime Minister Koirala did not lack the courage of conviction when it came to pursuing the course of action he had promised the people. In office the Nepali Congress made considerable efforts, within the framework of the ongoing first five-year plan, to attend to the exacting problem of reconstructing the country's traditional economy. The government gave top priority to the three most defiant problems of land, communication, and education. It was readily acknowledged that unless the land tenure system, the most patent cause of economic backwardness, was thoroughly reformed all efforts to revitalise the economy would be an exercise in futility. Few seemed to doubt the fact that revamping the economy hinged on a reasonable solution of the land problem.

Pursuant to its election pledge to the people, the ruling party took a sizable step forward when it announced its decision to abolish the tax-free *birta* system without any compensation. The regime also promised to establish rights for the tiller of the soil. Economic expansion was sought in other directions. An integrated system of education, including technical and medical, was put into operation. Efforts were made to expedite development projects such as river training, irrigation and power generation which had been included in the first five-year plan, scheduled to be completed in 1961. Taking one thing with another, the regime appeared to be inching its way forward towards its declared goals in domestic affairs.

In international affairs, the government's achievements were not to be made light of. Particularly significant was its approach to men and events in India. The manner in which Koirala handled Nepal's relations with India, considering his close ties with New Delhi, had much to commend itself. There is no gainsaying that not a few Nepalese looked upon him as India's man on the spot. Rightly or not, he was considered to be much too closely identified with the subcontinental milieu to follow an independent path of development. His performance however gave the lie to this.

His close personal relations with Nehru helped him appreciably to strike a good bargain not unoften. To quote one instance would suffice. Koirala was dead set on getting the India-Nepal trade and transit treaty concluded on as favourable terms as possible. According to him: "I got the message across to Mr. Nehru that what I wanted was an arrangement by which our goods should have an unlimited access to the Indian market. There should be no restriction, no duty. They mustn't levy import duty on our goods. But so far as Indian goods were concerned we should have the right to impose levy on them. I told Nehru that it was no doubt an unequal treaty, but if he was interested in Nepal's economic development he should agree to this.

"But the officers opposed this. They were very much opposed to this idea. On my visit to Delhi I discussed the issues with him. It was in 1960. He said: 'I am sorry, there was a hitch because they did not want this unlimited right of Nepalese goods into the Indian market.' But I said that that was the bulwark, that was the basis of our industrial policy, because we did not have a big enough home market for Nepalese goods at present. Of course it would not be always so. At least for some time we shall have to depend upon India for the marketing of the goods. Nehru said that 'as long as you are in the government—our friends in the government—there will be no difficulty.' I told him that you may be losing a few crores of rupees by this arrangement, (but) even if you do so because of this arrangement you will be strengthening our position, your friend's position in Nepal. Considering all these, it was a small price to pay. 'As long as you are Prime Minister and our friends are at the helm of affairs there would be no difficulties,' he reassured me. 'A few crores of rupees would not matter. But if some hardline party assumes power then they could disturb our economy.'

"I told him this is unlikely to happen. We are likely to win the next three elections or more. Then I said that I don't want to go back with empty hands to Nepal. He said, 'I would send for Jha [L K. Jha was looking after India's foreign trade] and you discuss with him.' I said it would be of no use unless he made up his mind and accepted my proposition. He said that 'you also try to convince Jha about it and I will not agree to anything that will disappoint you.' He sent for Jha and I discussed the matter with him. Before I left he came to see me at the airport early in the morning and told me, 'I hope you have got what you wanted." On the basis of the understanding he had reached with Prime Minister Nehru on his January 1960 visit to Delhi, Nepal got a new and relatively favourable trade and transit treaty with India in September.

This did not inhibit Koirala from judging issues pertaining to India-Nepal relations on their merits. His past political association with India or his personal preferences did not warp his sense of perspective. To illustrate the point, reference might be made to his reaction to a statement Nehru made on 27 November 1959 in a foreign affairs debate in the Indian Parliament. Nehru told Parliament that "any aggression on Bhutan or Nepal will be considered by us as aggression on India." Forthwith Koirala asserted that "Nepal is a fully sovereign independent nation. It decides its external and home policy according to its own judgement and its own liking without ever referring to any outside authorities. Our Treaty of Peace and Friendship with India affirms this. I take Mr. Nehru's statement as an expression of friendship that in case of aggression against Nepal, India, would send help if such help is ever sought. It could never be taken as suggesting that India could take unilateral action. Is there any apprehension of danger from any quarter? The answer is definitely no. We are at peace with everybody and we do not apprehend any danger from any quarter."

Referring to this in the course of his statement in the Rajya Sabha (Upper House of the Indian Parliament) on 8 December 1959, Nehru said: "If I mentioned Nepal on the last occasion, it was because over nine years ago there was a clear understanding between the Governments of Nepal and India on this point. It was no military alliance....I want to make it perfectly clear that this understanding has nothing to do with any kind of unilateral action on our part. We cannot do it, we will not do it....The Prime Minister of Nepal said something the other day on this subject, and may I say that I entirely agree with his interpretation of this question."

Koirala achieved a breakthrough in his dealings with China. Admittedly, China's interest at that point required that Nepal should be cultivated in view of the widening fissures in India-China relations. Still, he must be given his due for the imagination and initiative he displaped in approaching the task of putting China-Nepal relations on an even keel. At the earliest opportunity, in March 1960, he visited Peking to get the kingdom's border dispute with China out of the way, and that without meeting the Chinese request for a nonaggression pact and a road connecting Kathmandu with Lhasa. As Koirala told this author: "When I visited China...I said to Chou En-lai, it would be helpful if he could match their aid with that of India. Chou En-lai said: 'No, we do not want to compete with India.' He further said: 'It would not be good for you also. So our aid would be slightly less not because we cannot help you but because we do not want to appear to be competing with India."

When the author asked Koirala to elaborate on the non-aggression pact and the Kathmandu-Lhasa road the Chinese proposed to build, he said: "I told them that the road had no economic justification because it would not open up the valley to be developed economically. And that the trade between China and Nepal was not so heavy that it would justify the construction of the road. So I turned down that suggestion and said that the money...for the construction of the road could be utilised economically for a better purpose."

The issue cropped up again at Koirala's meeting with Mao Tse-tung. But the proposition was dropped when the Chinese found that the Nepalese were in no mood for it. As to why the Chinese mooted a nonaggression pact with Nepal, Koirala's "impression was that they wanted at that time to isolate India. India-China relations were not good at that time. They wanted to create an impression that, in the border dispute between India and China, India was in the wrong; China could settle its border disputes with Burma and all other countries. It was only with India—because of India's intransigence—that they could not come to an understanding. I think it was their purpose to diplomatically isolate India. They did not try to put undue pressure on me about the road construction (the Kathmandu-Kodari road) or the nonaggression pact. And they understood my resistance and my difficulties." Eventually he agreed to a Treaty of Peace and Friendship, which was formalised in April 1960.

But the regime's modest gains on the economic front were woefully inadequate to meet the rising aspirations of the people. Promises alone, no matter how radical, could not satisfy a people who had waited far too long for a break in the monotony of their wretched existence. They demanded some tangible evidence of the fact that the Nepali Congress meant business, that it was materially different from the other political parties that had been in power before. At another level, the opposition groups and parties were for a variety of reasons up in arms against the government. For one thing, being weak and divided, the opposition was ineffective. This made it irresponsible and abandon itself to the politics of expediency. For another, the ruling party's overwhelming majority in the legislature increasingly encouraged it to take things for granted, to assume a mien of arrogance and self-righteousness. This contributed to the growth of a climate in which the opposition seemed to care little for form, procedure, law or for policy as distinct from the politics of expediency.

Except the minuscule Communist Party, the other opposition parties denounced the government's land reform policy as one of "expropriation." The reforms measures also drew the wrath of not a few Nepali Congress members with a big-farmer background. The opposition groups and parties also had no reason to be pleased with Koirala's growing stature both at home and abroad. An additional arrow to their quiver was provided by the not quite negligible volume of corruption and administrative mismanagement. Reference might be made to what a not unfriendly critic of the Nepali Congress said a week after the King's take over. "The popular government was not effective and the administrative system did not make as much progress as required...Some of the Nepali Congress followers indulged in objectionable activities....Some of the ministers, especially the junior ones, were extremely indiscreet in accepting presents showered on them by the Russian Embassy. These included small cars, scooters and watches, and some senior civil servants also helped themselves, as they often do, regardless of the source.

The opposition was determined to exploit the situation not only to the disadvantage of the ruling party but also to its own eventual extinction. Deliberately ignoring objective conditions, the opposition groups and parties, including the Communist Party, declared a war on the government with no holds barred. It was not they alone who "clamoured for the resignation of the popular ministry. A section of the Nepali Congress led by M.P. Koirala jointed the opposition and demanded that King should save the country from the Congress 'dictatorship." Nepalese society doubtless could well do with purposive changes in every sphere of life. The multitude that lived, worked, reproduced and died in the hamlets, villages and towns were scraps of humanity which only evoked pity. They had yet to reach the stage when they would assert their right and refuse to take no for an answer.

With the opposition parties however it was an either—or issue, with nothing between. That is why they raised only one slogan—total opposition to the ruling party. Their theme song had only one bar: B.P. Koirala must quit the scene. If the chaff is winnowed from the grain, it would be seen that the opposition was firmly sold on the idea that political consistency was the virtue of lesser mortals but that personal equations were all that mattered in politics. Not that the opposition parties would not fight for democracy. It was just that they would do so according to their own rules, even if these were guided by nothing more ennobling than crass expediency. They could not "conceive of an opposition to the government which is less than total," failing to appreciate that "total opposition means revolutionary opposition, and revolutionary opposition, has to be prosecuted by conspiratorial and violent means." The opposition parties ultimately got what they had asked for—dismissal of the B.P. Koirala government. But they lost on the swings what they had made on the roundabouts.

Since King Mahendra was one of the two most important factors in Nepalese politics, his attitude to the functioning of the government needs study. In the initial stage the King extended considerable support to the government and the policies it pursued, including land reforms. Addressing the second session of both Houses of Parliament on 31 March 1960, he observed that "the administrative machinery of the country should be geared up to the need of a democratic government, and to this end different service cadres have to be organised. My government has been very effortful in this direction...The state being the ultimate owner of all land, my government has decided to bring to an end all feudal system, and the birta land...Being convinced that the success of true democracy can be measured only by the yardstick of the popular support available, my government has given higher priorities to local development activities and development boards on the district level are being formed...My government has been particularly attentive to convert our feudal society into an industrial society."

Koirala corroborated the fact that King Mahendra apparently chose to abide by the ground rules of the political game. He unreservedly admitted that the King stood by the government and the policies it pursued, not excluding land reforms. It was no miserly compliment to the King when

Koirala recalled that "whenever I discussed any point with the King he never disagreed. Never, not even once...When I inquired of him if he had any suggestion to make regarding the members of the Cabinet he said: "Well, you are the Prime Minister, it is for you to advise me. Whatever you suggest is all right for me." Among the many instances of the King's unequalified support to the government Koirala referred to his attitude to its "proposal to nationalise forest lands. The most affected persons were the King's family members. We said that we would make an evaluation of the land in terms of current price. Some difficulties arose over the quantum of compensation demanded by the princes, which was, according to us, unjustifiably high. Over this question also the King appeared to agree with us...Then there was the question of abolition of the feudal rajas. In Nepal there were large numbers of small principalities...The King did not object to that."

Time and circumstances seemed on the side of the Nepali Congress, notwithstanding the opposition's insistence on not playing the game. But the party was unable to make the best use of its opportunities. Intraparty feuds, corruption, jobbery and administrative inefficiency fast eroded the party's credibility. Allowing for the existing constraints, material and otherwise, it was not possible for the government to achieve spectular success. That this would bring grist to the mill of the government's critics and contribute to the emergence of pockets of discontent was in a way inevitable. But this was not half as significant as the party's refusal to face problems boldly instead of trying to dodge them.

Even eight years in the wilderness did not seem to have woken up the Congress leaders to the distressing fact that the Nepalese situation was farthest from what might sustain a democratic movement rooted in the soil, and the party had little that deserved to be called an organised mass following. As an admirer of the Congress observed in the correspondence column of a newspaper, "after coming to power as a result of the victory in the first general election the Nepali

Congress government was without any mass movement to back up its agrarian reforms and reforms in the sphere of administration." The leadership of the party failed to transform it into an ideologically sharp instrument that could have grapped with the task it had set itself at a meeting of its General Council in November 1958, "achievement of socialism through parliamentary democratic socialism under constitutional monarchy."

To expect King Mahendra to fail to take note of this would have been asking for the impossible. Rather he kept a close watch on developments and nothing of any import went unobserved. The general drift of affairs seemed to convey to him, as it did to many others, the impression that the Nepali Congress was caught in a cleft stick. In a public address at Banke-Bardia on 30 January 1960, King Mahendra rather sternly observed: "The fair name of democracy should never be permitted to be exploited to do evil rather than good to the people. It should never be allowed to create a climate where industries languish, rights and justice are difficult of access, bribery and other forms of corruption rife, unemployment increase, the people in the saddle should have all the loaves and fishes, and anti-national elements reap the harvest. The responsibility for all this has in a manner of speaking devolved on the entire Nepalese people too with their attainment of freedom."

The King cautioned his listeners not to relax their watch, not to take things for granted. Should the people of Nepal take no heed of what they were told, he said he might "be constrained to invite other actions in discharge of my duties and responsibilities." For he could not ignore the fact that he also had "certain duties by my country and these are to maintain the sovereignty of the country; to maintain national integrity; to improve our relations with other countries; to initiate actions oriented to the public good." He emphatically declared that if he found "any real let or hindrance along the path of my performance of these duties I would not hesitate to take whatever steps that may be necessary and at whatever cost...Let there be no misunderstanding on this score."

To give King Mahendra his due, he spoke his mind without any hesitancy. His message was precise. It was much too so for any intelligent Nepali, not to speak of the Prime Minister, to miss its import. He made it clear that the goings-on in the realm did not particularly impress him but filled him with anxiety on the contrary. There was also the hint that unless things changed in the desired direction he would act up to his reputation. But the King did not appear to have slammed the door shut on the democratic experiment as yet. If public pronouncements are any guide to one's thought's it would be difficult to call him anything but a democrat even as late as April 1960.

On the 29th day of that month the King was more than eloquent in his defence of democracy in addressing the National Press Club in Washington. He did not equivocate; he spoke with much feeling, and logically too. He observed that "in Nepal, as elsewhere in Asia, industrial revolution did not precede the political revolution. Nor could she have the direct advantages of the liberalisation of thought and humanisation of behaviour consequent upon change of outlook in matters concerning art, literature, thought and religion that could happen only in the course of what is called 'renaissance'.

"The other serious roadblock in the progress of democracy in countries like Nepal is that the age-old social and religious practices do not at all conform to the norms and standards of a modern democracy...Even such basic safeguards for a democracy as an independent judiciary, an independent audit and accounts department, free administrative cadres, a public service commission...even such basic safeguards for a democracy have to be built from scratch in Nepal...In my view, the yardstick for the success or otherwise of the democratic experiment in Nepal should be the measure of success or failure of the democratic institutions in doing away with the social and economic inequalities and encompassing the all-round development of the country...In the event of our failure to improve through the democratic institutions the living condition of the general public who have such deep faith in the efficacy of democracy and who would spare no pains for the advancement of the cause of democracy, [we] shall have to face a barrage of questions to be raised by those who subscribe to the alternation theories—I mean the communist theories—and shall have to undergo the misfortune of the possible accendancy of such thinking...a democracy should mean a process to advance the social, polititical and economic situation along the line of the majority opinion."

But Prime Minister Koirala had a different interpretation. In his judgement the King's protestation of faith in democracy was a smokescreen, no more. The fact was that he ran with the hare and hunted with the hounds, Koirala emphasised. He cited one instance to illustrate the point. According to him, although the King did not publicly oppose the abolition of the feudal principalities, he privately encouraged them to defy the government. This of course did not pose much of a challenge to the regime, the Gorkha incident excepted. On 25 October 1960 an "uprising" took place in the Gorkha district of West Nepal which, a government press note claimed, was engineered by men "masquerading as yogis under the leadership of Yogi Naraharinath." The yogi claimed that he was "the King's man, and what I am doing is that which the King wishes."

Referring to the incident Koirala said: "The King was not then in Nepal [he had gone to England on a state-cum-private visit] and Yogi Naraharinath, the agent of the King...was duly arrested...I was in India in connection with the student conference the All-India Nepali Student's Association had organised in Bombay...The yogi claimed that he had been asked by the King to do this and he showed some papers to say that he had been financed by the King...Now, he [the King] read in the London papers about my statement [regarding the incident] and was furious because I had involved him. Subarna was with him and the King told him: 'Look, Subarna, this is what your Prime Minister has said. And why should I be involved?'

"When he came back to Kathmandu there was an exchange of very hot words and he said: 'Why did you involve me?' I said: 'I did not involve you. I only said what the yogi exactly had been saying and had been brandishing some papers purported to have been sent by the Palace. We were thinking of prosecuting him for levelling this charge against the Palace and for instigating the revolt. To this the King said: 'But still I got involved.' Then I got a bit worket up and said: 'Your Majesty, you have been involved."

Answering the author's question whether the King was really a party to this incident, Kairala said: "Yes, I had proof of that —a letter written by his Military Secretary Malla to the yogi saying that in accordance with Maharaja dhiraja's command he was sending some money for his work, that he had been doing good work and Maharajadhiraja appreciated it and that whenever he needed money he might ask for it...He was arrested and the letter was found in his *jhola* (bag)...I went to the King and showed him the letter. He told me that he had given some money in charity. He also said: 'Can I not give some money in charity?' I said: 'Of course you can. But you 'must make sure what charity you are subscribing to. If by your charity an impression is created that you are being hostile to the administration, then you cannot do it. And it is not a simple charity, he is not a yogi doing some spiritual work. He was engaged in anti-state activity, everybody knew about it, and you were financing him. Your intention may be very good, but what whuld the people think about it?'

"He kept quite for a while and then said: 'Look, it appears both of us cannot be contained in the same place.' '...That was two days befere the coup. He said: 'Either permit me to fade out and you run the show as you like. Or you get out and let me rule as I think best. Both of us cannot be at the same place together.' Then I said: 'Your Majesty, this is a terrible statement you have made. I represent the people, you represent continuity, an institution; and you have certain political influence...It is in the interest of the country that both of us combine like two joined hands. And because the task of modernisation is beset with great difficulties I may humbly suggest, Your Majesty, even you should not be too confident, It would be a frightful boast on the part of Your Majesty that you can run it singlehanded, without the cooperation of the people, and modernise Nepal, Of course I cannot make that claim because it is a gigantic task, a national task which the nation as a whole has to fulfil.'

"And then he got up and said: 'Look, if you have any charge against me, do not give vent to that in public. You come here, see me and take off your shoes and beat me...'. I told him that the same thing applied to me. 'If I do anything that you consider harmful, you can send for me and do whatever you like. But as the King you should not criticise your government in public.' Then he got up, shook hands with me and sat down. And he sent for Malla, his Military Secretary. When Malla came he said: 'Malla, I have brought some gifts for B P. from England, and also for his wife. Bring them. "There were many gifts—a tape recorder, record player, bangles for my wife—and then he said: 'All right, put all these in his car.' That was the last meeting we had."

END OF AN EXPERIMENT

Between that encounter and the royal takeover barely 48 hours intervened. Did the Prime Minister take leave of his sovereign believing that all was right and that he had been able to mend the broken fences? Or did he leave the palace with two loads, presents from the King and worries about the time he would strike? Koirala was aware of the King's growing displeasure with the way the government was functioning. On his own admission, the Cabinet had earlier discussed the possibility of a royal takeover. Koirala had also been warned of the danger by more sources than one.

According to Koirala, "once Jawaharlalji told me, as the American industrialist Henry Ford had told me earlier, that there were reports that the King had another kind of thinking... He said: 'In the interests of Nepal both of you should combine.

We want to see that no difference crops up between the King and you.'" Even the US President, General Dwight Eisenhower, whom "I meet...in September or October 1960...said that 'if there was any difference between you and the King, you should try to make that up because Nepal needs both of you."

The present author also felt, on a visit to Kathmandu about a month before the takeover, that "parliamentary democracy is a very latecomer on the political stage of Asia. In Nepal it arrived only yesterday and, candidly speaking, its roots lie rather...exposed on the surface...The institution of monarchy constitutes a very influential factor in Nepal's political life...the King is not nonpartisan in the sense it is understood in, say, Great Britain. The Palace wields an amount of direct influence that cannot fail to affect the functioning of the government... parliamentary democracy rests on a rather delicate mechanism in Nepal."

Still Prime Minister B.P. Koirala seems to have left the palace more or less assured that the King's gesture was not unfriendly. There could be two plausible explanations of his conduct: either he had become overconfident and started believing his charisma would enable him to emerge victor in any confrontation with the King. Or he had become a fatalist, concluding that it would be pointless to make any efforts to reverse the process. The impending tragedy could not be averted because, the Prime Minister reasoned, he did not have a grass-root, ideologically oriented and disciplined organisation to do it. He did not seem to have been alive always to the fact that "the success of the [democratic] experiment depended on co-operation between the King, who derived his position of leadership and authority from the time-honoured institution of monarchy," and himself, "who symbolised popular hopes and aspirations but had yet to create popular tradition and institutions to sustain his democratic passion and ideas."

Here was the problem. The leadership of the Nepali Congress was unable to rise to the occasion. Although Koirala was aware of the inherent weakness of his position and the strength of the King's, he failed to see his way to grasp the nettle. Inconsequential defails of everyday administration claimed his time and energy, much to the detriment of the party. The inability to reorganise the party, and build such voluntary institutions as would have a stake in pluralist democracy increasingly inclined Koirala "to take the easy way out by giving in to charisma to cut the Gordian knot of difficulties." The point appeared to have been missed that charisma and rationality stood poles apart. Also, because of historical reasons and in the given context, the King stood an immensely better chance of outplaying him in this game of charisma.

One of the major shortcomings of the Nepali Congress was its failure to realise that the "problems of nation-building and social development" required it "to direct human motivations from old forms of activity to newer ones," which only an ideologically revamped party could have engineered. This was not to be Koirala sought to make up for this by his one-man campaign a give a socialist facade to the party. Also, to preserve his revolutionary ideology and integration. It is another matter that this did not arrest the process of destabilisation of the party. To the extent that intraparty conflict intensified, some of his trusted colleagues became articulate in questioning his difficulties in the opposition outside grew louder, and the difficulties in solving the basic problems of food, shelter and clothes multiplied, Koirala's reliance on charisma increased. So did his appeal to socialism.

In point of fact, even as the palace guards were on their way to arrest him he was discoursing on democratic socialism to a gathering of the valley's students and youth. On the morning of 15 December 1960 Koirala went as scheduled to inaugurate the first general conference of the Nepal Tarun Dal (Nepalese Youth Organisation).

His message to the assembly of people was that the country would never be theirs until they could free it from the course of feudalism. He urged them to work for the cause of democratic socialism. For this alone could ensure a society where man would cease to be the object of exploitation by man, a society that the earth's wretched and the poor could call their own. He remained his audience that democracy and socialism were inseparable, and he promised to ensure that democracy would not be strangled in the name of socialism. Nor would he permit exploitation to continue in the name of democracy. He emphatically declared that the Nepali Congress stood resolutely committed to democratic socialism. That was the last that the people of Nepal heard from their first elected Prime Minister before the King's men took him prisoner.

King Mahendra is dead. He is no longer around to argue his case. And not many, Nepalese or others, would be willing to do that if for no other reason than at least to avoid being identified as defenders of the wrong cause. It is not intended here either to hold a brief for him. Still, to set the record straight, it would be necessary to understand, if that is at all possible, the reasons that might have ultimately prevailed upon the King to take the plunge. Of them three stand out: (a) feeling of uncertainty; (b) a desire for total political power, and (c) an obsession with destiny.

The King was not a relaxed person. A feeling of insecurity took a fast hold of him. That fear was of an individual and not of the multitude. Nor of the political parties, including the Nepali Congress. True, he did not have much patience with the party system, but that was more because he had empirically observed that the parties had neither the grit and stamina nor the courage of conviction to act according to their instructed judgement. He could well perceive that the parties had not outgrown their juvenile state of amorality and unreason. Their approach to the problem of democracy was essentially conditioned by empiricism of the worst sort. Devoid of a sense of perspective, empiricism in their case was seemingly a passport to accepting expediency as the guiding principle in politics. The tone and temper of Nepalese politics was far from what could meet the total requirements of the given task—democratically developing Nepal's underdeveloped society in the shortest possible time.

King Mahendra was not afraid of the politicians, except one. He knew he could get most of them to bend to his will. But B.P. Koirala made him uneasy. The Prime Minister's utterances and doings were a constant reminder to him that the sovereign was one of the factors, and not the only factor, in Nepal's power equation. Koirala also reminded him of Jung Bahadur, and of Mohammed Mossadegh before his ouster. The King could not with equanimity watch Koirala's growing charisma, his nonchalance, his increasing predilection for referring to himself in the third person singular. It was not Koirala's increasing reference to socialism that unnerved him but the fear of losing his own political initiative. In Koirala's repeated emphasis on the concept of constitutional monarchy the King detected the threat of being denuded of the substance of power. There was the fear of the monarchy being relegated to the position it had occupied between the mid-19th and mid-20th centuries, and of its becoming a prisoner of a commoner prime minister instead of hereditary Ranas.

At no point after the end of Rana rule had King Mahendra either as Crown Prince or sovereign indicated that he was not irrevocably reconciled to the concept of "the system of power... as a moving balance of many competing interests." Rather he had not infrequently given the impression that in his "conception of Nepal's political future," as J.P. Narayan told the author, "the sovereign is the ultimate repository of power, and that must remain so. Whatever freedom, whatever constitution, whatever steps toward freedom are to be taken are all gifts by the sovereign to the people."

Reduced to its essentials, the King's concept of the power structure was a pyramid. Whatever his political rhetoric, he had consistently sought a system of polity that would not question the fact that the Palace constituted the nodal point in the kingdom's power srructure. Those who occupied prime ministerial office before the first general election did not dispute this attitude. They came and went just as he would have them do. But B.P. Koirala, the first Prime Minister to enter Singha Durbar with a mandate from the people, fell into heresy. He raised questions, a few too many for the King's liking. Worse still, he refused to recognise the monarch as the keystone of the power arch.

King Mahendra had a heightened sense of destiny. That was the lesson of history he had learnt only too well. While myths told him that the King of Nepal was an incarnation of Vishnu, history revealed that the institution of monarchy possessed a certain element of indestructibility. In its journey across time it had weathered many internecine feuds and conflicts. Also rebellions and wars. It survived all this because destiny had so ordained. To King Mahendra, Nepal was an idea, and none but he could realise what it was destined to be.

History strengthened his belief. No less so did the prevailing conditions of life within and outside the country. Even a cursory glance at a map of Asia or Africa seemed to feed him on his mystique. Over the wide horizen that stretched from the Sea of Marmora to Manila Bay, encompassing a multitude of peoples and cultures, he noticed the lengthening shadow of a political way of life that did not conform to the system of life and ideals parliamentary democracy symbolished. In that segment of the world, where more than one half of its total population lived, the democratic system of politics had been tried and found wanting. Or so it seemed to him. Of course there were exceptions. For example, India, Malaysia, Japan and Israel. But they only proved the rule.

More relevant to his line of thinking were the experiments with political system building in two very populous and problem-ridden countries of Asia. The concept of "basic democracy" and that of "guided democracy" which Presidents Ayub Khan and Sukarno had introduced in Pakistan and Indonesia respectively appeared to him to be the right answer to the political problems the developing countries faced. They gave him his cue. If Nepal was to be rescued from the spreading tentacles of poverty, bad government, corruption and social dissension, if it was to be saved from disintegration, more, if it was to have a place in the sun, it needs must have a rallying point, a catalytic agent. And what could constitute this but the monarchy, King Mahendra concluded his argument.

The two clashed, and the King triumphed. The royal takeover was a solution of sorts to the kingdom's political problems which had been building up over the years and which had acquired a complex dimension because B P. Koirala was apparently found either moving too fast for, or lagging too far behind, the people. Mahendra's action was not a *coup d'etat* in the semantic sense of the term. It was a takeover effected within the bounds of the kingdom's Constitution. In exercise of the powers enumerated under Article 55 of the Constitution, the King acted, and he had the support of a sizable number of politicians of diverse persuasions, including some leading members of the Nepali Congress.

Apparently the Congress had all along been skating on thin ice. The absence of any spontaneous and immediate reaction to the takeover was indicative of this. It might be suggested that the King's solution for these problems of politics were not future-regarding. But, then, every problem, as Lenin put it, has two solutions—a progressive and a reactionary. If revolutionary forces fail to accomplish a given task and find a revolutionary solution, history will not wait. It would see to it that the problem finds a solotion, progressive or otherwise.

One thing is plain. The solution largely reflected the King's belief, not unlike that of the crowned heads in 18th century Europe, that "progress came from above, reaction from below, and that Kings and queens were as liberal as their diets were conservative." It seemed nothing could shake his conviction that the monarchy provided a national focus, that it alone was in a posision to break the stranglehold feudalism had put on Nepalese society. That is, the institution of monarchy was exclusively privileged, historically and otherwise, to steer the ship of state clear of the disintegrating forces of obscurantism, casteism, regionalism and linguism. The institution of monarchy was "the chief constructive principle of the state," and it would have to ensure Nepal's emergence as an integrated polity much in the same way as the Bourbon rulers of France waged their fight against provincial particularism. So far, so good. But there is no knowing whether King Mahendra pondered over the contigency that history might not repeat itself all along the line. It might not allow Nepal the time it given the Bourbons before the storming of the Bastille.

APPENDIX A

Text of the Threaty of Peace and Friendship Between the Government of India and the Government of Nepal, 1950

The Government of India and the Government of Nepal recognising the ancient ties which have happily existed between the countries for centuries.

Desiring still further to strengthen and develop these ties and to perpetuate peace between the two countries.

Have resolved therefore to enter into a Treaty of Peace and Friendship with each other, and have, for this purpose, appointed as their plenipotentiaries the following persons, namely.

The Government of India

His Excellency Shri Chandreshwar Prasad Narain Singh, Ambassador of India in Nepal.

The Government of Nepal

Mohan Shamsher Jung Bahadur Rana, Maharaja, Prime Minister and Supreme Commander-in-Chief of Nepal.

Who having examined each other's credentials and found them good and in due form have agreed as follows:

Article 1: There shall be everlasting peace and friendship between the Government of India and the Government of Nepal. The two Governments agree mutually to acknowledge and respect the complete sovereignty, territorial integrity and independence of each other.

Article 2: The two Governments hereby undertake to inform each other of any serious friction or misunderstanding with any neighbouring state likely to cause any breach in the friendly relations subsisting between the two Governments.

Article 3: In order to establish and maintain the relations referred to in Article 1: The two Governments agree to continue diplomatic relations with each other by means of representatives with such staff as is necessary for the due performance of their functions.

The representatives and such of their staff as may be agreed upon shall enjoy such diplomatic privileges and immunities as are customarily granted by international law on reciprocal basis provided that in no case shall these be less than those granted to persons of a similar status of any other state having diplomatic relations with either Government.

Article 4: The two Governments agree to appoint Consuls-General, Consuls, Vice-Consuls and such consular agents, who shall reside in towns, ports and other places in each other's territory as may be agreed to. Consuls-General, Consuls, Vice-Consuls and other consular agents shall be provided with exequaturs or other valid authorisation of their appointment. Such exequatur or authorisation is liable to be withdrawn by the country which issued it, if considered necessary. The reasons for the withdrawal shall be indicated wherever possible.

The persons mentioned above shall enjoy on a reciprocal basis all the rights, privileges, exemptions, and immunities that are accorded to persons of corresponding status of any other state.

Article 5: The Government of Nepal shall be free to import, from or through the territory of India, arms, ammunition or warlike material and equipment necessary for the security of Nepal. The procedure for giving effect to this arrangement shall be worked out by the two Governments acting in consultation.

Article 6: Each Government undertakes, in token of the neighbourly friendship between India and Nepal, to give to the nationals of the other, in its territory, national treatment with regard to participation in industrial and economic development of such territory and to the grant of concessions and contracts relating to such development.

Article 7: The Governments of India and Nepal agree to grant, on a reciprocal basis, to the nationals of one country in the territories of the other the same privileges in the matter of residence, ownership of property, participation in the trade and commerce and other privileges of a similar nature.

Article 8: So far matters dealt with herein are concerned, this treaty cancels all previous treaties, agreements and engagements entered into on behalf of India by the British Government and the Government of Nepal.

Article 9: This treaty shall come into force from the date of signature by both Governments.

Article 10: This treaty shall remain in force until it is terminated by either party by giving one year's notice.

Done in duplicate at Kathmandu this 31st day of July 1950

(Sd) Chandreshwar Prasad Narain Singh,
For the Government of India.

(Sd) Mohan Shamsher Jung Bahadur Rana,
For the Government of Nepal.

APPENDIX B

Text of Article 55 of the Constitution of the Kingdom of Nepal, 1959

(1) If His Majesty in his discretion is satisfied that a grave emergency exists whereby the security or economic life of Nepal, or any part thereof, is threatened by war or external aggression, or by internal disturbance, he may by proclamation in his discretion:

(a) declare that his functions shall, to such extent as may be specified in the proclamation, be exercised by him in his discretion;

(b) assume to himself all or any of the powers vested in or exercisable by Parliament or any other government body or authority;

and any such proclamation may contain such incidental and consequential provisions as may appear to him to be necessary or desirable for giving effect to the objects of the proclamation, including provisions for suspending in whole or in part the operation or any provision of this Constitution:

Provided that nothing in this clause shall authorise His Majesty to assume to himself any of the powers vested in or exercisable by the Supreme Court or to suspend, either in whole or in part, the provisions of Part VI of this Constitution.

(2) Any such proclamation may be revoked or varied by a consequent proclamation.

(3) A proclamation under this article, other than a proclamation revoking a previous proclamation, shall cease to operate at the expiration of twelve months, but may be

renewed by a further proclamation, and so forth until His Majesty is satisfied that grave emergency no longer exists.

(4) Any law made by His Majesty under powers assumed by him under this article shall, unless sooner repealed or re-enacted by him, cease to operate at the expiration of six months after a proclamation under this Article has ceased to operate.

(5) In exercising his powers under this article, His Majesty shall so far as may be practicable act after consultation with the Council of State.

WHAT IS THE NEPALI CONGRESS?

The Nepali Congress is a political party formed to establish democracy and restore fundamental rights to the people putting an end to the oligarchy.

The formation of the Nepali Congress took place in January 1947. It was then known as the Nepali National Congress. Later, it merged with the Nepali Democratic Congress to form the Nepali Congress in March 1950. The Nepali Congress is a broad based organisation, which awakens a new spirit in the entire people and marches ahead in league with them.

B.P. Koirala was the main architect of the basic principles and the policies of the Nepali Congress. It is an well organised party with village, district and central committees. Top ranking leadership of the Nepali Congress is composed of the Supremo Ganesh Man Singh, President Krishna Prasad Bhattarai, General Secretary Girija Prasad Koirala and a central committee of 24 members.

It is a common forum for intellectuals, professionals, peasants, workers, war-veterans, students and all the men and women of progressive outlook.

The Nepali Congress membership is of two categories:

(i) ordinary (ii) active

All Nepali citizens who believe in democracy, embrace socialism and yearn for nationalism, can become its ordinary members.

Its active membership is entitled to those workers who are regular and dedicated to the cause of social service, and recommended by the district committee. Only do the active members deserve the right to contest elections.

The Meaning of Jai Nepal

Jai Nepal is a slogan of the revolution of 1950-51. This is an outcry against the self-centred tyrants who ignored the interests of the motherland. To greet a comrade by saying Jai Nepal is to wish success or victory to all the Nepalis including peasants and workers. It is a greeting of equality. Jai Nepal is a symbol of Nepali national awakening.

Nepali Congress Flag

The Nepali Congress Flag flutters on vertical position, with two horizontal red bands and white band in the middle with four red stars. The upper and lower red bands signify political and socio-economic revolution. Middle white band symbolises peace and progress. Four stars are known for freedoms:

—Freedom of speech and expression.

—Freedom of faith, belief and worship.

—Freedom from want and protection against hunger.

—Freedom from fear, coercion and servitude.

Performance of the Nepali Congress

Concerned with the welfare of the industrial workers, the Nepali Congress led workers' strike in Biratnagar in 1947, which was first of its kind in the history of Nepal. It has always been lending its support to the cause of the workers ever since.

The Nepali Congress led the revolution of 1950-51 and liberated the country from Rana autocracy which culminated in the first experiment in democracy in Nepal.

In order to benefit the peasantry of Nepal, the Nepali Congress initiated an attack on the feudal system of land holding. It has been waging a relentless struggle in the interest of tenants.

The Nepali Congress introduced social reforms such as providing equal rights to women, removing untouchability and ploughing land by brahmins.

The Nepali Congress raised the banner of revolt against the political oppression and economic exploitation and remained active in eliminating social discrimination over since its inception.

The Nepali Congress led revolution of 1950-51 heralded a new era in Nepal. This unleashed a renaissance in the sphere of education, health, industry, commerce and laid a firm foundation of nationalism.

The Nepali Congress established independent judiciary, public service commission and modernised administrative system.

In December 1957, the Nepali Congress launched and successfully led a country-wide civil disobedience movement demanding early elections to facilitate formation of a popular government.

In the General Elections on the basis of universal adult suffrage of February 1959, Nepali people sumptuously restored Nepali Congress to power.

The Nepali Congress won 74 of the 109 seats in the House of Representatives and its great leader B. P. Koirala became the first elected Prime Minister of Nepal.

Despite its short 18 months in office, the Nepali Congress government accomplished great tasks with an unprecedented sense of economic equality and social justice.

A sense of direction was imparted to the development of the villages and the uplift of small farmers with the introduction of 'Village Development plan' and 'Cooperative Movement.

Guided by the consideration "To ensure every Nepali family a standard of living including food, clothing, housing, education and medical care within 15 years" the Nepali Congress was making great efforts.

In order to realize the cherished goal of economic progress, a Five-Year Plan was being prepared.

The Nepali Congress abolished Birta System (feudals owning rent free land) and Rajya courts (relics of the feudal past).

The Nepali Congress nationalised the fallow land and forests owned by the feudal lords.

It introduced land reform measures and guaranteed tenancy rights to the cultivators.

It codified the Muluki Ain (Law of the Land) and started levying taxes in a socialistic order to uplift the poor.

It established the Royal Nepal Airlines Corporation. The Nepali Congress took a daring initiative to open schools throughout the country. It established Tribhuvan University and encouraged to open new college of liberal arts, science and teacher education. Then Deputy Prime Minister Subarna Shumshere was the first Vice-Chancellor of the University.

Bearing in mind the fact "The improvement of transport is the backbone of country's development" a regional transport organisation was set up for the implementation of road projects. Priliminary survey works were undertaken for construction of East-West Highway and extention of ropeway facilities. With the operation of internal air services, far flung villages were no more remote. Communication systems were modernised. Survey works for several hydro-electric projects were completed.

To pave way for technology transfer to the peasants, scientific methods were adopted in the field of agriculture. Irrigation projects of different magnitude were implemented. Actually, the Nepali Congress gave cells like "produce more grains" and "go to the village and take care".

Cottage industries and industrial areas were encouraged under government subsidy and patronage in various parts of the country. Preliminary works in regard to the establishment of Birgunj Sugar Factory, Janakpur Cigarette Factory and National Trading had been Completed. Thus in industry and trade sector, the Nepali Congress government emphasised the prominent role of public sector also along with small cottage industries and private investment. It announced a two fold increase in the payscales for administrative and the army personnel. Further, Employees Provident Fund Corporation also came into existence.

It expanded her diplomatic relations to enhance the prestige of the country and became active participant on the international arena.

B. P. Koirala government's foreign policy, with full faith in the United Nations, was indicative of Nepal's vigorous search for a distinct national identity.

This government was extremely popular and Koirala's prestige rose high on the international scene.

Movement for Restoration of Democracy

When democracy was throttled on December 15, 1960, Nepali Congress alone resented with upsurge and took to arms twice.

It motivated student movements, championed the voice of the small farmers, workers and warveterans and supported the just struggle of teachers. It played a crucial role in the mass movement of 1979 and the referendum of 1980 in favour of multi party system.

It launched nationwide historic Satyagraha against the totalitarian regime in June 1985. Eight thousand activists courted arrest.

It started signature campaign and staged demonstrations against unemployment, pricerise, scarcity, smuggling, exploitation and corruption prevalent under panchayat regime.

It observed "mass awakening week" in September 1989, as a rehearsal before the proposed mass movement. Its workers met with draconian security acts and inhuman torture even while planting the saplings, donating blood and cleaning public places. The saplings were uprooted. But the party remained firm and resolute.

Despite heavy odds, the historic three day national convention was held in January 1990. The Nepali Congress sounded its bugle for launching a mass movement to end the panchayati reign of terror, to restore multiparty democracy and to conduct free and fair elections to a parliament by an all party interim government.

The historic party convention highly boosted the morale of the people. The people reposed their faith in the political force of the Nepali Congress. The Nepali Congress successfully led the mass movement and restored multiparty democracy plus the human rights in Nepal and got promulgated the new democratic Constitution of 1990 with constitutional monarchy and with the people of Nepal as the repository of power.

In its long and arduous struggle to restore democracy several hundred Nepali Congress workers have attained martyrdom. Some were buried alive. Some were hacked to pieces. Some were hanged to death. Some fell to the bullets. Some were blown to the smithereens. Thousands were incarcerated for many years. Thousands have been made disabled. Thousands were forced into exile. Thousands were deprived of their properties. Thousand families were shattered.

Though, without caring a straw for these numerous torments, brave fighters of the Nepali Congress have been contantly struggling and are prepared for any sacrifice in the service of the nation, as and when the situation warrants.

Policies and Programmes

The Nepali Congress, the kingdom's largest party held a three-day conference in Kathmandu's stadium on January 19-21, 1991. Attended by 15,000 party activists from all parts of the country, it was inaugurated by the party president, Shri Krishna Prasad Bhattarai, who is also Prime Minister in the interim Government. The party used the occasion to discuss draft of its election manifesto.

The Nepali Congress released its election manifesto on March 14, 1991. The party reiterated its faith in democratic socialism.

Sisters and Brothers

On the eve of the historic General Elections taking place in a democratic Nepal, the Nepali Congress greets Nepalese people from all walks of life. The party extends its heartfelt tributes to those martyred during our long democratic struggle. The party also congratulates and felicitates the young generation of and above the age of 18 which would be participating in the free elections for the first time.

Nepali Congress' Commitment: Democracy and Human Dignity

The Nepali Congress believes that the people are the greatest and most decisive force in a country's politics and governments, they are not revenue paying subjects but the real masters of a nation. They are not a force to be ruled by a government but the force to be served by the govenment.

The Nepali Congress wants to establish a political system and a practice of economic development oriented towards bettering the life of the farmers and workers who constitute majority of our population and toil most but still do not have enough to eat and wear. The party commits itself for protecting and promoting multi-party democracy, constitutional monarchy, people's sovereignty and their fundamental human rights. Therefore, by winning the people's confidence the Nepali Congress wants to:

— promote nationalism,

— establish the practice of free and impartial democratic electoral process,

— promote the decisive role of the people in the country's politics and the dignity of the House of Representatives,

— make the government and administrative machinery of the country honest and committed towards the people,

— establish and promote rule of law and an independent judiciary,

— establish freedom and impartiality of the press and the media.

Our View of Democratic Socialism and Development

The principal objective of the Nepali Congress' democratic socialism is to improve the lot of the rural poor, women, children, helpless old persons, backward communities and those living in dire poverty. Development is not only a mechanical process calling for the investment of capital and technology but is essentially a social and political process to organise and mobilize the people. Hence Nepali Congress believes that economic development is not possible without democracy. The Nepali Congress is resolved to raise the income of the people-the rural poor, workers, landless small entrepreneurs, people with limited income, teachers and civil servants and ex-service men, women, people of old age, and people of backward and oppressed communities to a level adequate enough to meet their housing, fooding, educational, health and entertainment expenses.

The Nepali Congress which believes in democratic socialism for the country's economic development wants:

— to ensure the prosperity of the country and the people through mixed economy,

— to remove hunger, disease, and poverty through equitable distribution of national product,

— to ensure the participation of labour in production management,

— to develop a culture ensuring equal dignity and rights to all the people,

— to establish social and economic parity by reaching prosperity and the government's services to the oppressed and poor people,

— to ensure social security for the old, disabled and helpless people by providing them pensions adequate enough to live a respectable life.

Rural Development

— The overall development of the country is not possible without the uplift of villagers and rural populace. The Nepali Congress would therefore invest a minimum of 70 per cent of the resources and development outlay available with the government for rural development.

— It would create income and employment opportunities at the village level by establishing small cottage and agro-based industries.

— It would create income-oriented activities for small farmers, women, and people of backward communities promoting vocational training by opportunities in various skills.

— Free educational facilities will be extended up to secondary level in the rural areas.

— Would ensure the supply of pure drinking water in all the villages within ten years.

— Would electrify all the villages.

— Would open fair price shops.

— Would conduct rural housing projects to settle the people in an organised and orderly manner.

Land, Agriculture and Farmers

— Nepali Congress would ensure the right of the tiller. The party would develop an appropriate policy to do away with the present dual ownership of land.

— The party would encourage peasants farming within prescribed land ceiling and would impose progressive taxation on those farming in more than the prescribed ceiling.

— The Party would attract the capital and human resources land to away from productive industries and services.

— Would distribute the land available with the government among the landless and settle them in an organised way.

— Would make available seeds, fertilizers, pesticides, appropriate technology and other agricultural services to the farmers at their doors.

— Agricultural loan would be made available on easier terms. The practice of charging high interest rates on such loans would be dispensed with.

— The role of cooperatives would be made effective.

— Policies to fix reasonable prices of agricultural products and their procurement would be formulated.

— Groundwater and surface irrigation facilities would be widely expanded. Appropriate measures to control flood, landslide etc. would be taken.

— A policy and programme to establish fertilizer industries in the country within five years would be formulated to meet domestic needs.

- Special concession would be provided in the consumption of electricity, petrol, diesel etc. in agricultural sector. The policy to conserve the environment through the use of electricity, bio-gas and solar energy would be adopted.
- Facilities relating to veterinary care centres, quality feed and fodder would be made available for quality livestock farming.
- Programmes relating to farming of useful crops, fruit cultivation or livestock farming would be conducted in the Terai, hills and mountains depending on topography and climate.
- Laws would be enacted to outlaw the feudal system of bonded labour.

Industry and Trade

- Nepali Congress would encourage the growth of cottage, small-scale and agro-based industries.
- Labour intensive industries requiring low investment of capital would be encouraged.
- Industries based on domestic resources and generating more employment opportunities would be encouraged.
- The widespread inefficiency in government undertakings would be done away with.
- The private sector would be encouraged to participate in the growth of industry and commerce by providing protection to capital and investment.
- Necessary protection and encouragement would be given to foreign capital investments and joint ventures.
- The practice of black marketing smuggling and corruption in the trade sector would be effectively eliminated.
- Trade deficit would be controlled by discouraging imports of luxury goods and boosting exports.

— Export of products reflective of indigenous skill and craft fetching better prices in the international market would be encouraged.

— Import of commodities of daily necessity of the common people and those needed to promote export oriented industries that generate more employment would be encouraged.

— Formalities relating to international trade would be made easier and efficient.

— Internal trade would be developed and expanded in the rural and hill areas to provide relief to the people by resolving supply constraints and controlling prices.

Education, Teachers and Students

— Nepali Congress would establish one university each in eastern and western Nepal within three years.

— A policy would be adopted to make available primary education opportunity to all the children within ten years. Arrangements would be made to enable the children to receive education in their own languages upto the primary level.

— A campaign on free adult education would be launched to eradicate illiteracy within ten years.

— Free education up to the secondary level would be ensured in a stepwise manner. The quality of higher education would be improved and access to it made easier with stress on equal opportunity.

— Educational curriculum which would compliment rural development would be developed.

— An employment oriented educational system directed towards developing human resources in the areas of professions, science and technology would be developed.

— Necessary approvals would be accorded and compensation rendered to schools opened or proposed in the private sector.

— Scholarships and necessary facilities would be extended to girl students and students belonging to backward communities.

— Sanskrit education would be made more scientific and employment oriented.

— The youths in the country would be encouraged to participate in cultural and sports activities along with education.

— The professional rights, interests, dignity and respect of teachers would be protected and promoted.

Health Services

— Nepali Congress would formulate a programme to extend health services to all the Nepalese people within the next ten years.

— Immunization services would be expanded. Health care centres would be established in every village and primary health services would be extended free of cost.

— Education on sanitation would be spread through out the country. "Cheap, clean toilets" would be introduced.

— Arrangements would be made to make available pure drinking water in all rural and urban areas in the country within the next ten years.

— District hospitals would be properly equipped.

— Ayurvedic medical system and the research and processing of herbs would be encouraged.

Rights and Welfare of Children

Nepali Congress would formulate a programme to reduce child and infant mortality rate by 75 per cent within the next ten years. It would thus ensure their right to live by protecting them from preventable death.

Transport

— Nepali Congress would link all the 75 districts with road transport network within the next ten years.

— Air transport would be developed and expanded in remote and hill areas.

— Roads would be constructed to interconnect villages in the Terai and hills and link them with national highways.

— Electric railways and trolley bus services would be introduced wherever possible from Mechi in the east to Mahakali in the west.

— Water transport would also be developed. The construction of ropeways would be encouraged.

— Bridges, suspension bridges and culverts would also be constructed and proper arrangements would be made for the repair and maintenance of roads.

— Environmental conservation would be primary consideration while developing the transport secror.

Communications

— Nepali Congress would formulate policies and programmes to ensure the freedom of the communication media.

— People's right to information would be prosected.

— Telephone and wireless services would be expanded to all district headquarters, bazaars, big settlements and, depending on necessity, to villages within the next ten years.

— Efficient postal services would also be introduced in each village development committee.

- New transmission centres for Radio and Television would be established and programmes would be broadcasted in regional languages as well.
- A policy would be adopted to enable the press and communication media in the private sector to develop as an industry.

Foreign Policy

- Democracy, human rights and commitment towards world peace would constitute the main plank of Nepali Congress' foreign policy.
- Nepali Congress would advocate the sovereignty, national integrity and independence of each nation. The party would express solidarity in all peaceful struggles against apartheid and communalism.
- The party believes that mutual problems between two nations should be resolved through peaceful negotiations and that solutions should be sought within the parameters established by the United Nations.
- The party is against the expansion and piling of nuclear arsenals.
- Nepali Congress believes in active non-alignment, world peace and an effective role of the United Nations.
- The party advocates regional understanding and wants the South Asian Association for Regional Cooperation (SAARC) to play an effective role.
- The Nepali Congress believes in greater friendly relations with both the big neighbours: India and China.

Foreign Assistance

- Nepali Congress would formulate policies and programmes to invest foreign assistance in priority areas to be ascertained by the country and not by the donors.

— Foreign grants would be used in projects relating to agriculture, education, health, population control and environmental conservation.

— Foreign loans would be invested in production-oriented and foreign exchange earning industries and services.

— Policies would be framed for greater mobilisation of domestic resources.

— Bilateral and multi-lateral private investment would be encouraged in order to import necessary capital and appropriate technology.

Water Resources Development

— Nepali Congress would formulate policies and programmes to exploit the country's abundant water resources to electrify all villages and hamlets.

— National income would be increased and the peoples standard of living raised by exporting surplus electricity.

— Electricity based transport services would be developed.

— The consumption of firewood, diesel, petrol etc, would be reduced to safeguard public health and to conserve forests and protect the environment.

— Small hydro-electricity projects would be undertaken for rural electrification.

Tourism Development

— Nepali Congress would formulate a detailed programme to develop all of the country's natural, cultural and historical spots into tourist areas within the next five years.

— Tourist services and facilities would be expanded to the district level instead of confining them to urban areas only.

— Policies and programmes would be formulated to attract tourists towards the Nepalese way of living and consumer goods in order to check the outflow of tourist earnings.

— Tourism development plans would be formulated in such a way so as not to pollute the country's socio-cultural traditions and the environment.

Population Control

— Nepali Congress would accord high priority to population control and population control education programmes in the country.

— Effective programmes would be formulated to mobilize peoples voluntary participation to reduce the existing high fertility rate in the country.

Price Control

— Nepali Congress would resolve existing supply constraints and inflation by resorting to various means such as increase in production and services, improvement in distribution system and control of black marketing.

— Policies and programmes would be formulated to resolve, with immediate effect, the existing supply problems and uncontrolled price rise in the hills and remote areas of the country.

Forests and Environment

— Nepali Congress would resort to rationale use of forest resources to make available firewood and timber to the people.

— Forests would be preserved not by using the force of police and military but through people's cooperation and trust.

— Afforestation programmes would be undertaken as a national campaign.

— Policies would be formulated to encourage forestry and afforestration in the private sector.

— Wildlife would be preserved.

— Community participation would be mobilised in protecting the preserved forest areas.

— A "Forest Army" would be raised to make the people aware of the significance of forest resources and their preservation.

— A policy to preserve the country's environment and forest resources from pollution and destruction would be adopted while formulating economic development plans.

Mines and Natural Resources

Nepali Congress would undertake necessary survey, research etc. to efficiently and scientifically exploit the existing natural resources in the country.

Urban Development

— Nepali Congress would resolve the existing urban problems pertaining to the supply of pure drinking water, sewerage etc.

— Urban transport would be regulated and the facilities expanded.

— The cleanliness of the city areas would be ensured and the environment preserved.

— Residential and industrial areas would be developed separately, roads constructed, afforestration undertaken, parks and places of entertainment constructed and the pollution from vehicles effectively checked to keep the cities clean and protect the environment.

Women's Uplift

— Nepali Congress would formulate policies and programmes with the conviction that the respect and uplift of women is the starting point of the country's development.

- Policies to provide equal treatment before law and special encouragement in education and employment would be adopted.
- Programmes would be formulated to reduce the high mortality rate of mothers by 50 per cent within ten years. Health services would be expanded to check malnutrition and to increase average life expectancy.
- Effective legal action would be taken and social campaigns launched to check women trafficking.

Workers

- Nepali Congress would adopt policies to enable the workers to get appropriate wages, bonus, allowances and medical facilities.
- Policies and programmes would be formulated for the participation of workers in production management.
- Legal measures would be undertaken to guarantee the professional rights, interests, employment and dignity of the workers.
- Workers unions would be duly accredited and representations made in concerned areas.
- Districtwise arrangements would be made for skill development and technical training.
- Appropriate labour policies would be adopted to enable retired workers to lead a respectable life.

Landless and Unemployed

- Nepali Congress would resolve the problems pertaining to the landless and the squatters at the earleist.
- Arrangements for resettling the landless would be undertaken after compiling a scientific record of the actual landless people.

— Employmant opportunities would be made available to individuals and families not able to make a living from agriculture.

— Employment opportunities would be expanded in the areas of construction, education, health and services by imparting vocational and technical education and through necessary skill development trainings to resolve the problems relating to unemployment. Employment opportunities would also be expanded in trade, industries and in the private sector as well. Employment exchanges would be established to regulate the demand and supply of personnel.

Civil, Police and Military Service

— Nepali Congress will adopt policy to guarantee job security and to safeguard the professional rights and interest of those employed in civil, police and military services.

— The party's policy would be to respect and protect the efficiency and the self-respect of all the employees.

— Nepotism and favouritism would be effectively done away with.

— Opportunities for the appropriate administrative and management education and training would be made available.

Justice for All

— Nepali Congress would develop a free, impartial and efficient judicial system for all.

— Free legal service would be provided to the poor and needy.

Income Slabs and Taxation

— It would be the policy of Nepali Congress to extend facilities to the people with low salary and income.

The government would constitute Commissions from time to time to evaluate and ascertain salaries.

— Nepali Congress would adopt a policy to impart social justice through progressive taxation.

— Affluent people escaping taxation so far would be subjected to tax.

— Tax paying habit would be encouraged. Reforms would be introduced to check tax leakage.

— Income and urban property taxation system would be made practical uncomplicated and efficient.

— Adhocism in taxation system would be done away with.

— A Tax Commission would be constituted to revamp the present tax structure.

Decentralization and Local Development

— Nepali Congress would entrust the people their rights through the decentralization of power.

— Village, town and district level autonomous units would be made powerful and efficient in accordance with the policy of decentralization.

— Judicial, administrative, educational and health facilities would be expanded to the local level.

Public Service Commission

— The Public Service Commission would be made free, impartial and efficient and its services expanded to the district level.

— Provision would be made for writing in alternative languages in PSC examinations to do away with the community and language constraints of the candidates.

Ex-Servicemen

— Nepali Congress would ensure the representation of ex-servicemen in various political bodies.

— Programmes would be launched to employ and settle ex-servicemen in various trades and professions according to their skill and efficiency.

Art, Literature, Culture and Science

— Nepali Congress would ensure the development of autonomous and independent academies of literature, fine arts, culture and science for their growth.

Martyrs and Political Sufferers

— Nepali Congress would honour those martyred during democratic struggles and undertake welfare programmes to benefit their families.

— A record of political sufferers would be compiled and they would be appropriately honoured.

Excesses of the Panchayat Era

— Nepali Congress would initiate of legal action against those responsible for killing the people and for committing administrative, financial and political abuses during the Panchayat era.

Community and Regional Problems

— People from different regions, caste and communities would be inducted in civil, police and military services without discrimination.

— Different languages, culture and traditions existing in the country would be preserved and promoted.

— A development process would be adopted to eliminate regional and community differences.

Special Programme for Remote Areas

— Special programmes would be implemented in remote mountain areas to make the local inhabitants life comfortable. Arrangements will be made to supply foodgrains and essential commodities in such areas.

Religious Freedom

— Nepali Congress will adopt a policy to allow every Nepali citizen to profess the religion and rituals of one's conviction.

— Monuments of religious and historical significance—temples, monasteries, mosques etc.—would be preserved and renovated.

Miscellaneous

— Loan up to Rs. 5,000 made available to earthquake victims would be written off.

— Prisons would be improved and educational and employment oriented programmes implemented to reform the prisoners.

— A policy would be adopted to provide relief to the users of electricity in accordance with the consumption and status of the user.

— Market prices and supply of foodgrains, sugar, kerosene etc. would be controlled and regulated.

— Anti-social activities like abuse of authority, black marketing, smuggling, drug abuse and trafficking etc. would be sternly dealt with and checked effectively.

Presenting these programmes and its resolve to the people, the Nepali Congress entreats people from all walks of life to vote the Tree, its election symbol, to victory.

Vote the Nepali Congress for peace, stability, welfare and development and to put an end to poverty and suppression and to eliminate disease and illiteracy.

Select Bibliography

Buchanan, Francis, *An Account of the Kingdom of Nepal and other Territories Annexed to the Dominion by the House of Gorkha*, Edinburgh: Constable, 1819.

Caplan, Lionel, *Land and Social Change in East Nepal: A Study of Hindu-Tribal Relations*, London: Routledge and Kegan Paul, 1970.

Chaterji, Bhola., *A Study of Recent Nepalese Politics*, Calcutta: World Press, 1967.

Chaudhuri, K.C., *Anglo-Nepalese Relations, From the Earliest Times of the British Rule in India till the Gurkha War*, Calcutta: Modern Book Agency, 1960.

——, *Constitution of the Kingdom of Nepal*, New Delhi: Nepal Trading Corporation, 1950.

Gupta, Anirudha, *Politics in Nepal: A Study of Post-Rana Political Developments and Party Politics*, Bombay: Allied Publishers, 1961.

Hagen, Tony, *Nepal: The Kingdom in the Himalayas*, Berne: Kummerly and Frey, Geographical Publishers, 1961.

Horwitz. I.L., (ed.), *Power Politics and People: The Collected Essays of C. Wright Mills*, New York: Oxford University Press, 1963.

Husain, Asad, *British India's Relations with the Kingdom of Nepal, 1857-1947: A Diplomatic History of Nepal*, London; George Allen and Unwin, 1970.

Imam, Zafar, *World Powers in South and South-East Asia: The Politics of Super-Nationalism*, New Delhi: Sterling Publishers, 1972.

Jain, Girilal, *India Meets China in Nepal*, Bombay: Asia Publishing House, 1959.

Joshi, Bhuwan Lal and Rose, Leo E., *Democratic Innovations in Nepal: A Case Study of Political Acculturation*, Berkeley, University of Callifornia Press, 1966.

Khatri, Padma Bahadur, *Nepal's Foreign Policy*, Kathmandu: Department of Information, Ministry of Communications, His Majesty's Government, 1972.

Koirala, Bishweshwar Prasad, *Nepal Tarun Dalko Pratham Mahadhibeshanma Dinubhoiko Udghatan Bhasan*, Kathmandu: Gorkhapatra, 1960.

Kumar, Satish, *Rana Polity in Nepal: Origin and Growth*, Bombay: Asia Publishing House, 1967.

Landon, Perceval, Leys, Colin (ed.), *Nepal*. London: Constable, 1928, 2 vols. *Politics and Change in Developing Countries: Studies in the Theory and Practice of Development*, Cambridge University Press, 1969.

Lohia, Rammanohar, *Fragments of a World Mind*, Calcutta: Maitrayani, (n.d.).

Mahendra, His Majesty King, *Proclamations, Speeches and Messages*, Vol. 1 (July 1951-December 1960). Kathmandu: Department of Publicity, His Majestry's Government, 1967, Tr. by Damen R. Tuladhar, Vol. II (December 1960-1965). Kathmandu: Department of Publicity. His Majesty's Government, 1967.

Mihaly, Eugene Bramer, *Foreign Aid and Politics in Nepal: A Case Study*, New York: Oxford University Press, 1965.

Narayan, Shriman, *India and Nepal: An Exercise in Open Diplomacy*, Bombay: Popular Prakashan, 1970.

Nehru, Jawaharlal, *India's Foreign Policy: Selected Speeches, September 1946-April 1961*, Delhi: The Publications, Division, Government of India, 1961.

——, *Panchayat Democracy*, Kathmandu: Department of Information, Ministry of Communications, His Majesty's Government, 1972.

Pant, Y.P., *Planning for Prosperity in Nepal*, Kathmandu: Nepal Cultural Association, 1957.

Pant Y.P. and Jain S.C., *Long-Term Planning for Agriculture in Nepal*, Delhi: Vikas Publishing, 1972.

Regmi, Dilli Raman, *Modern Nepal*, Calcutta: Firma K.L. Mukhopadhyay, 1961.

Rose, Leo E., *Nepal: Strategy for Survival*, Berkeley: University of California Press, 1971.

Rose, Saul, *Socialism in Southern Asia*, London: Oxford University Press, 1959.

Russell, Bertrand, *Power: A New Social Analysis*, London: George Allen and Unwin, 1939.

Shaha, Rishikesh, *Nepal and the World*. Kathmandu: Khoj Parishad, Nepali Congress (National Congress Association), 1955.

——, *Nepali Politics: Retrospect and Prospect*, Delhi: Oxford University Press, 1975.

Shrestha, B.P., *Economy of Nepal*, Bombay: Vora and Co. 1967.

Shumsher, Subarna., *A Report to the Nation: Press-Radio Interview (Series Two)*. Kathmandu: Department of Publicity and Broadcasting, His Majesty's Government, 1960.

Tuker, Francis., *Gorkha: The Story of the Gurkha of Nepal*, London: Constable, 1957.

Wright, Daniel, *History of Nepal*, Cambridge University Press, 1879.

